ENDORSEMENTS

"Michael Pink's Book, "GOD'S [...] come to us at the right time with [...] entrepreneurs toward the pinnacle of their dreams. It is so packed with insight that I read it twice to absorb the content and I recommend it without reservation. I cannot think of another "self-help book" that equals it!"
Dr. Peter J. Daniels, International Statesman, Prolific Author, Founder of the World Centre for Entrepreneurial Studies

---

"This foundational masterpiece is deep! It's actually four books in one and is filled with practical business strategies and proven business models, all encoded in the Scripture. It's nothing short of amazing! With easy-to-apply formulas and step-by-step instructions, this book contains over 100 life changing secrets - and it only takes one to change your life. We cannot recommend this highly enough."
David & Jason Benham, Best-Selling Authors, Nationally Acclaimed Entrepreneurs

---

"Father's success secrets are throughout the Bible and in all of His creation; Everything He does is wired for success. The absolute amazing news about all that, is that Father uniquely gifted and called Michael Pink to gather and reveal the natural, spiritual, social, and relational truths for success for His Body in this age, at this time. If you have a career, a business, and/or a ministry, then owning, consuming, and continually referencing this book is essential to your success!"
Rick Osborne, Best-Selling International Author, (over 110 million books in print) Publisher, Speaker and Bible Teacher

"Wow! I'm blown away. A masterpiece, this could be Michael's best book yet. It is a gift to the world of business and the body of Christ. Thank you for emptying yourself for our benefit."
Patrice Tsague, Author -Biblical Entrepreneurship

Why are things the way they are? This primary question is on the minds of everyone, from CEOs to managers, from professionals to artisans, from adults to kids. We all yearn to understand the world and our place in it. With alacrity and precision Michael Pink gives us not just the answer but the secrets to the power behind the question. He takes what many just pass by in the busyness of the day and shows us the fingerprints of God hidden in plain sight that help renew our faith, give our dreams flight, and show us that what we most hope is true about life, creation and our destiny is in fact not only possible but inevitable.

It's as though Michael has given us night vision goggles to see the very DNA of God's thoughts and ways embedded in creation and ready for us to put to good use in the here and now. Humbling. Energizing. Powerful. If you want to operationalize your vision, start reading this book now.

Eric Beck, CEO, Expert Ownership, LLC

"You were born with the heart of William Wallace… As one of America's Greatest Teachers and Evangelists with a destiny to knight businessmen and women in the army of God. It is an honor to know and learn from you. You are one of my hero's."
John Beehner, CEO, Wise Counsel

"Michael has given us an extraordinary book that combines the natural and the spiritual to reveal God's Best Kept Secrets that will allow you to gain incredible insights into the nature of God in a way that will allow you to apply them in your business life for success as well as all areas of your life. Michael has an uncanny ability to connect the spiritual laws with the natural laws of nature. Your life will be enriched by reading and applying the principles revealed in this book. Well done Michael!"
Os Hillman, author TGIF Today God Is First, President of Marketplace Leaders

---

"Michael's knowledge, his understanding and ability to convey deep Scriptural truths applied to businesses at any level is unsurpassed. Whether you read and apply just one chapter or drink from his firehose of 101 Bible-based, wisdom-filled business strategies, your business will be realigned with Kingdom principles at every level. Follow the inexhaustible principles written here and in a very short time your business will prosper."
Wally Kassebaum, Friend, Online Business-Growth and Logistics Consultant

---

"Your application of Biblical principles is without equal, and you easily motivate us to use them in our daily lives. You are a truly inspiring teacher, and we are blessed to have you as a friend and an educational mainstay of the NACFC" (National Association of Christian Financial Consultants).
Mark Minnella, President, NACFC

"Having studied your content for several years, I am thrilled to see you release this book. It is so needed, especially in today's climate where commerce is now an obvious spiritual battlefront. God's Best Kept Secrets is the most comprehensive biblical business book ever written. It's literally a graduate level success manual for every business leader. Every Christian business owner should own this book as a daily reference guide, and it should be a textbook at every God-fearing business school."
Tim Porter, Founder, God's Business Revolution

Michael Pink has had a profound impact on my life, family, business, and outreach. His calling is empowering God's people to take back the gates of commerce. Michael is the world's foremost authority on Biblical Strategy and Natural Law for sales and business. God has given Michael an uncanny gift to be able to extract practical success principles (God's wisdom) for life and business from familiar scriptures. He is a phenomenal writer and master communicator, expressing the heart of the Father.

God's Best Kept Secrets is a WOW book—the culmination of the most important secrets (principles) the LORD has revealed to Michael during his life. Reading any one of the chapters will inspire you. Reading the book will absolutely transform your life and business.

Joseph Peck, M.D. The Time Doctor
Founder and President of Empower 2000

GOD'S BEST KEPT SECRETS

BOOK ONE

TAKING BACK THE GATES OF COMMERCE
Walking With God – A Game Changing Strategy

MICHAEL Q. PINK

Hidden Manna Publishing

Other books by Michael Q. Pink

Biblical Business
The Divine Blueprint, The Race is Not to the Swift, The Perfect Business Model, The Bible Incorporated, Selling Among Wolves, Rainforest Strategy, 7 Secrets of the Sale

Christian Living
The Words in Red, Tough Questions – Straight Answers, Psalm 91 - The Ultimate Shield, The Lord's Prayer – Amplified, His Little Instruction Book, Promises Worth Keeping, The Armor of God, The 23rd Psalm, The Beatitudes, The Comforter, Grace for Grief

---

GOD'S BEST KEPT SECRETS
BOOK ONE: *Taking Back the Gates of Business*
by Michael Q. Pink

Published by Hidden Manna Publishing
A Michael Pink Innovations entity

This book or parts thereof may not be reproduced in any form, stored in a retrieval system, or transmitted in any form by any means – electronic, mechanical, photocopy, recording, or otherwise – without the express, prior written permission of the publisher, except for brief quotes with attribution and as otherwise provided by United States of America copyright law.

Copyright © 2022 by Michael Q. Pink
All rights reserved

Cover Design by Mark Herron of MR Herron Productions

ISBN: 9798834613725

ACKNOWLEDGEMENTS

This book would not exist if it were not for **Jesus Christ**. He is my Lord, my Savior, my confidant, and my closest friend. He welcomes my prayers and speaks to me like a friend to a friend, even closer than a brother.

He also gave me **Judy Ann** after losing my wife of 24 years to illness. She is my strongest supporter, my beloved, the one in whom my heart completely trusts. She is my voice of reason and the love of my life.

To **Peter J. Daniels**. Wealthy by any measure, Peter Daniels took the time to stay in touch and share his secrets with me. For that, and for his friendship, I am forever grateful.

To my lifelong friend, **Rick Osborne**, who more than anyone I know has pursued intimacy with God and been used by God at pivotal times in my life to secure my destiny in Him.

To **Wally Kassebaum** who has come alongside me and helped fill the void in technology knowhow. I am grateful for his faithfulness and friendship.

Lastly, I want to acknowledge the hundreds of thousands of men and women around the world who have bought my books, training, and coaching programs over the years. You are my inspiration and the reason I put in the effort. Thank you for your support!

CONTENTS

BOOK ONE: TAKING BACK THE GATES OF COMMERCE
Walking With God – A Game Changing Strategy

Acknowledgements
The Key to Everything (Preface)
1. Taking Back the Gates of Commerce
2. First Things First
3. Walk with God – A Game Changing Strategy
4. The Bible: God's Instruction Book for Life and Business
5. Thinking the Thoughts of God
6. How to Defeat the Giants in Your life
7. The Coming Wealth Transfer – Not Quite What You Think
8. The Generosity Factor
9. Discover the Genius in You
10. How Freshly Poured Wax Can Save Your Business
11. The Power of Now
12. Godly Indignation: Rocket Fuel for Your Business
13. Destroying the Yoke with Prosperity
14. The Necessity of Desire
15. Hesitation – The Killer of Dreams
16. The Power of Understanding: How to Get it & Why it Matters
17. Mercy and Truth – The Unfair Advantage
18. Imagination: The GOD CARD
19. Problems are Your Provision
20. The Bigger Your Problem, The Bigger Your Opportunity
21. The Lies We Believe Are What Hold Us Back
22. Seven Wealth Building Secrets of Isaac

23. Faith That Actually Works
24. All Things Are Possible, or Was Jesus Just Kidding?
25. You Only Think You've Been Trusting God
26. Never Give Up – Taking Back What's Been Stolen
27. Miracle Restoration
28. Nice Guys Can (And Should) Finish First
29. The Mustard Seed Fallacy
30. Finding Abundance Right Under Your Nose
31. The Rule of Three for More Effective Communication

Last Word

OTHER BOOKS IN THIS SERIES...

BOOK TWO – The DIVINE BLUEPRINT
Biblical Models for Succeeding in Sales & Business

1. The Moses Questioning Strategy
2. Negotiating Secrets of the Apostle Paul
3. Presentation Strategies of the Apostle Peter
4. God's Divine Blueprint for Success in Life & Business
5. Seven Marketing Secrets Discovered in the Scroll of Isaiah
6. God's Success Formula
7. The Great Business Commission
8. The Three Step Persuasion Process Jesus Promised
9. How to Change Your Life Forever
10. High Probability Selling (Parable of the Sower)
11. Selling Among Wolves
12. Sixteen Qualifications for Corporate Leadership
13. Gaining Market Domination
14. Three Battles Every Leader Must Win

15. Communication Secrets of Jesus – Know Your Stuff
16. Communication Secrets of Jesus – Identity Shifting
17. Communication Secrets of Jesus – Word Pictures & Illustrations
18. Communication Secrets of Jesus – The Power of Story
19. Communication Secrets of Jesus – Speak with Authority
20. Communication Secrets of Jesus – 4 Ways to Establish Credibility
21. Communication Secrets of Jesus – Be Substantive
22. Communication Secrets of Jesus – Passion, Mystery, Contrast

BOOK THREE – THE RACE IS NOT TO THE SWIFT

Unlocking the Mystery of Perfectly Timed, Divinely Orchestrated Happenings

1. The Race Is Not to The Swift
2. Good Luck Favors the Prepared
3. The Ultimate Shortcut – Discovering The "et" of God
4. Timing Trumps Everything
5. Outshine Your Competition - 17 High-End Service Strategies
6. Belief and the E.A.S.Y. Close Sales Process
7. Make Your Value Proposition So Compelling, People Will…
8. A Winning Formula for Creating Unbeatable Offers
9. Binding the Strongman of False & Limiting Beliefs Increases
10. The Proper Use of Bonuses and Guarantees
11. The Ephesian Model to Win Over Your Market
12. The W.A.S.P. Memory Method
13. Gaining High Resolution Clarity for Accelerated Growth
14. Vision Gives Pain a Purpose
15. Lead with Speed
16. Leverage Through Others
17. Top Ten Reasons Businesses Fail

18. How Incremental Improvements Bring Monumental Increase
19. Seven Laws of Multiplication - PROFITABILITY
20. Seven Laws of Multiplication - VELOCITY
21. Seven Laws of Multiplication - FREQUENCY
22. Seven Laws of Multiplication - SCALABILITY
23. Seven Laws of Multiplication - FEASIBILITY
24. Seven Laws of Multiplication - PROBABILITY
25. Seven Laws of Multiplication - LEVERAGABILITY
26. Twelve Secrets for Developing a Winning Mindset

BOOK FOUR
The PERFECT BUSINESS MODEL
7 Natural Laws For Success!

1: God's Perfect Business Model
2: Seven Success Secrets of a Tree
3. Everything Starts with a Seed
4. Seven Success Indicators for Startups
5. Four Indicators for Picking the Right Market
6. Three Primary Nutrients Every Startup Must Have
7. Three Secondary Nutrients for Building a Sustainable Business
8. Micronutrients for Maximum Success – God is in the Details
9. Business Runs on Water
10. Connect to the Power of Light
11. The Warmth Factor – How Intensity Moves the Needle
12. Problems Are your Provision CO_2
13. Seven Success Habits of Trees Every Business Needs to Emulate
14. The Only Two Things That Can Kill Your Business
15. The Hidden Cost of Pests Can Sink You
16. Seven Natural Strategies to Maximize Productivity

17. Defeating the Pathogens That Defeat You
18. Flower Power – How to Make Your Offer Irresistible
19. Seven Laws of Natural Marketing
20. The Seven Phases of Growth
21. Seven Roles Every Business Must Fill
22. Brazil Nut Effect - How to Profit Without Cash

THE KEY TO EVERYTHING
(Preface)

I was shipwrecked…
Nearly 40 years ago, my life was on the rocks. I hadn't been in church much in the previous four years and decided to visit a church where I didn't know anyone.

I drove up in my late model Chevy station wagon (compact version) after the service had started and looked for a vacant parking spot behind the church.

As I made my way between cars to the back entrance of the church, feeling slightly uncomfortable about meeting people, I passed by the driver's side of an older Datsun (now Nissan) station wagon. There was nothing notable about this car, but for reasons I couldn't understand, my eyes were drawn to the driver's side keyhole for the car.

It looked completely normal, yet it was as if I was being told to look hard at that door lock.

I stopped, stared at the keyhole, and couldn't fathom why I would be prompted to notice and pay attention to it.

I wasn't a "woo woo" kind of guy. I didn't attach meaning to random things, yet there it was, an indelibly strong impression to pay attention to, and remember that keyhole.

Moses was drawn to notice and approach a burning bush that wasn't being consumed by the flame. (Exodus 3:3) I can understand why he would stop and check that out, but this looked completely normal and boring, so after closer examination, I shrugged it off, questioned my sanity, and went in the church.

When the service was over, I filed out the back door, keeping to myself, walking past that same car, paying it no attention as I made my way to my car some 20 – 30 yards away. Just as I got my key out to unlock my car, I heard a voice calling out… "Sir… Sir… Can you help me?"

I didn't turn around at first because I was sure he couldn't be speaking to me. After all, the parking lot was full of people going to their cars and he was probably calling out to one of them. But he persisted. So, I turned and asked what he wanted.

He explained that he was the owner of that Datsun station wagon I had eyed on the way into church, and that he had accidentally locked his keys in the car and was nervously wondering if the key to my station wagon would unlock his door. (After all, both cars were station wagons.)

I politely explained that my car was a much different year, make and model. In fact, our cars were produced on two different continents, separated by an ocean and about 10 years in age. I was certain that my key would never unlock his door. But he persisted.

As if to prove my point, I acquiesced and walked over to the driver's side of his car, slightly annoyed, put my key in the door and turned it. To my utter astonishment, my key unlocked his door as if it was made for that door!

He was thrilled, thanked me profusely as he gleefully retrieved his keys from the driver's side floor mat, and I walked away a little dazed by the experience. I didn't realize it at the time, but

God was training me to recognize his promptings and to act on them, regardless of how unusual they may seem.

In the decades that followed, I asked God what that was all about. He helped me to understand that He was giving me keys from His Word and His creation, to unravel mysteries and solve problems for seemingly impossible situations, and help folks get back in the game, overcome incredible odds and fulfill their destiny in God.

I've used those keys to work with startups, insolvent companies, and Fortune 100 corporations. In every case, those keys have worked wonders, bringing some back from the brink of disaster and helping others to simply punch through barriers that had previously been impenetrable to them.

For some, it was about personal and radical transformation as they gave their lives to Jesus. For others, it was about business transformation like transforming a failing commercial real estate company who had lost 75% of their sales team, helping them become the fastest growing real estate brokerage in America and the 16th fastest growing, privately held company on the INC 500 list.

This book series puts those keys on full display. It reveals for the first time, many of the secrets and insights God has given me over the last 36 years that have helped tens of thousands improve their lives.

Instead of a handful of insights, I created a set of four books that are a virtual cornucopia of God's wisdom, curated into **101 chapters** that collectively have literally hundreds of powerful strategies for life and business.

Think of them as keys. And it only takes one of them to unlock your destiny and get you on track to maximize your God given potential.

Think of this set of books as a reference series, which means you can literally start reading at any point in any of the books. Just find a topic that is of interest and/or speaks to a need you have and begin there. No need to start in chapter 1 if what you need most is a sales process found in chapter 6 of Book Three.

Book One (Taking Back the Gates) was written as a matter of honesty. It would be dishonest of me and disloyal to my Savior not to share the **Spiritual Laws** that resulted in amazing outcomes that will blow you away.

I included this book because succeeding in business apart from a deep and abiding relationship with Jesus Christ is pointless. Plus, I wanted to share ways in which you can activate your faith to bring about seemingly miraculous results.

Book Two (The Divine Blueprint) is all about **Biblical Models**. It's the idea of copying God, by modeling your business activities after patterns found in Scripture.

Whether it's the Negotiating Secrets of Paul, the Presentation Strategies of Peter, the Moses Questioning Strategy, or the Divine Blueprint in Exodus, there is so much to be gained by applying the wealth of wisdom they model for us.

Book Three (The Race is Not to the Swift) is all about **Practical Strategies** for building and strengthening your business. Whether outlining a proven, step-by-step sales process, making a compelling value proposition, making unbeatable offers, or seven different ways to multiply your profits, this section will give you immediately useable strategies to grow your business.

Book Four (The Perfect Business Model) reveals the hidden wisdom of God found in **Natural Law** that He built into His creation. How I discovered it and what you will learn will astound you. If you love God, are intrigued by science, and enjoy business, you'll love Book Four.

While I did my best to pack as much value in the four-book series as I could, so you could really run with the wisdom it contains, there is so much more I'd like to share with you.

That's why I created a private mentorship group where I am making available (free to members) hundreds of hours of training videos where you can go much deeper on many of these topics.

Learn more at MichaelPink.com/Secrets

CHAPTER 1

Taking Back the Gates of Commerce!

"That in blessing I will bless you, and in multiplying I will multiply your seed as the stars of the heaven, and as the sand which is upon the seashore; and **YOUR SEED** *shall possess the gate of his enemies."*
(Genesis 22:17)

"They blessed Rebekah and said to her, 'Our sister, may you be the mother of thousands of ten thousands, and **let YOUR SEED possess the gate of those who hate them**.*'"* (Genesis 24:60)

"If you are Christ's, then **YOU ARE ABRAHAM'S SEED** *and heirs according to the promise."* (Galatians 3:29)

War is at our gates.

Many portals of power have already been captured.

Do we want to be trampled under the foot of our enemies or possess the gate of our enemies as promised in Scripture?

If we abandon the Biblical mandate to serve and lead in the gate, we will be conquered, ruled, and led!

What are the gates?

They are the centers of power and influence in a nation. They control what is allowed in and out of a country. The gatekeepers of our time control companies like Facebook, Google and Twitter, who combined own more than 300 companies like YouTube, Instagram, WhatsApp, and Motorola.

They sway election outcomes, limit your access to information, tell you what to believe and drastically limit free speech.

But then there's the big six media companies (Comcast, Disney, Time Warner, News Corp, National Amusements and Sony) who according to Business Insider magazine, control 90% of the radio, print, television, and entertainment media in America.

Think of it... Nine entities sit atop the gates of commerce and decide what they will allow you and me to see, hear, say, and experience. That's a lot of influence. They may not literally control what you can say, but they control the platform from which you can be heard, and they can shut you down on a whim, wiping out what may have taken you years to build.

And there are no appeals.

Just think... In the 1880's, the New York Times was owned by evangelicals and was the leading pro-life voice in America referring to abortion as "child killing". Imagine the impact if it came into the hands of godly stewards again. Imagine if CNN became an honest, reliable, and trustworthy voice. It may soon be for sale again. Anyone interested?

How did it happen that we allow men to compete as women in sports or make it ok to allow boys to use the girls' bathrooms in school? How is it that 2nd graders are being taught that pornography is normal or that there are many different genders for them to choose from.

Why did it become okay to teach CRT (Critical Race Theory) built on the intellectual framework of identity-based Marxism to school children?

When the printing press came along around 1436, the first book printed was the Bible. Religious literature was the primary use of that technology. When the internet came along, the first and biggest success story was pornography and has become the technology of choice for pornographers ever since.

Have we lost our mind?

How did this and a hundred other ills I could mention come to be the norm? I think the answer may be found in Judges 5:8… *"**They chose new gods;** **Then was war in the gates:** Was there a shield or spear seen among forty thousand in Israel?"*

America has chosen new gods and literal war is near to our gates. The question asked in Judges 5:8 indicates a lack of courage and leadership in Israel. Never has America had a weaker leader than we now have. Our nation, and in many respects, the world, is in grave danger.

It's time to take back the gates of influence currently under the sway of Hell itself. Jesus said, *"I will build My church and **the gates of Hell** will not prevail against it."* (Matthew 16:18) Think about that passage… The gates of Hell are NOT defensive gates. They are the power centers of influence in our culture that are **arrayed against us**, but in the end, Jesus said, they will not prevail against the church.

We tend to think of gates as physical structures that allow or deny entrance into a city or perhaps a private community or home. While that is true, biblically speaking, gates represented the seat of authority for three things.

1) Civil / Political Leadership
*"And the king of Israel and Jehoshaphat the king of Judah sat each on his throne, having put on their robes, in a void place **in the entrance of the gate** of Samaria."* (1 Kings 22:10) When world leaders want to meet about something, where they meet is a big deal. The meeting place always communicates a message.

In the case of the kings of Israel and Judah, the gates of the city were seen as highly important and symbolic. So much so, that they had their physical thrones transported to the gates to sit on and conduct their summit from. It is understood that he who controls the gates, controls the city and thus the gates represent the various seats of authority.

Today, in America, government has taken for itself authority that goes well beyond national defense and the biblical mandate for government found in Romans 13 which is to *"do good and execute wrath on him who does evil"*.

It has now extended itself to things like health care (including unconstitutional mandates) and education that teaches our children what to think, not how to think.

Additionally, government through the granting of tax-exempt status, now asserts control even in religious matters such as messaging (what you're allowed to say or restricted from saying) from the pulpit, and in recent times, regulating if and when they can meet, and how many are allowed to attend services!

2. Judgment / Judiciary:
*"Then shall you bring forth that man or that woman, who has done this evil thing, **to your gates**, even the man or the woman; and you shall*

stone them to death with stones." (Deuteronomy 17:5) People were brought to the gates to receive judgment.

In today's world we see how the judiciary has intruded heavily into family matters, redefining what a family is, how many genders there are, legalizing abortion and even attempting to limit one's ability to protect themselves and their family. There is a full-on assault on the family structure.

3. Commerce / Finance:
"Then Elisha said, 'Hear ye the word of the LORD; Thus saith the LORD, Tomorrow about this time shall a measure of fine flour **be sold for a shekel, and two measures of barley for a shekel, in the gate of Samaria.***"* (2 Kings 7:1) Commerce was conducted at the gates and according to Ruth 4, even real estate deals were closed at the gates.

The gates of commerce represent the place where fortunes are made. And as they say, "He who has the gold, makes the rules." Some who currently dominate the gates of commerce have leveraged their resources to control what you see, hear, and read through the media conglomerates they control.

Those dominant players at the gates of commerce reach into every sphere of life to influence it according to their preferences. Where governmental authority is needed to get their agenda through, they just need to set apart 10% for the "big guy" and everything will be fine, or so it was said on Hunter Biden's laptop.

Money gives you influence. Look no further than Bill Gates who in 2006 had Chinese president Hu to his home for dinner – BEFORE he met with President Bush. Then in 2015 Gates had a private meeting with President Xi in Seattle. Maybe both

Chinese presidents were just exchanging their favorite sushi recipes with him, but then again, world domination might have been part of the discussion.

While influence gained through wealth can be used for evil, it can also be used for good. Joseph of Arimathea used his influence to meet with Pilate and secure the body of Jesus. (Mark 15:43) Why not set your sights on big things that can influence our generation and those coming behind us, for good? Let's quit griping about the evil and get on the field and take some ground!

I'm not expecting Christians to rule the world. I believe what Jesus said that the wheat and tares will grow up together until the harvest. (Matthew 13:30). Then, at harvest time, according to Jesus, the tares will be gathered first and burned, and then the wheat will be gathered into His barn. Read that passage slowly and consider the ramifications.

The thing about wheat and tares is that they compete for the same resources. That means the ground we want to take will be contested. Fiercely. But we are well able because *"greater is He that is in us, than he who is in the world."* (1 John 4:4)

Solomon said, *"wisdom is a defense"*. (Ecclesiastes 7:12) The word for defense is most often translated as "shadow" as in *"He who dwells in the secret place of the Most High shall abide under the **shadow** **of the Almighty**."* (Psalm 91:1)

For there to be a shadow, there must be something casting that shadow. If the shadow leaves, the object casting that shadow must also have left.

Do you remember when the 12 spies returned from checking out the Promised Land? Joshua and Caleb reported this about the enemy… *"Their defense is departed from them,"* (Numbers 14:9) The word translated as defense in this verse is the same word usually translated as "shadow".

Shadows implied protection. Money is like that. It can be used to purchase protection from anything from cold and hunger to security and legal representation.

Obviously, God is first and foremost our protection, and He can provide food for the hungry in miraculous ways. He did that with the loaves and fishes, but don't forget that Jesus also had a treasurer who kept the money bag. He used both the natural and the supernatural to meet needs.

Solomon went so far as to say, *"Money answers all things"* (Ecclesiastes 10:19). In today's vernacular, you might say, "Money talks". Wisdom excels money and that is beyond dispute both biblically and observationally, but Solomon observed, *"the **poor man's wisdom is despised, and his words are not heard**."* (Ecclesiastes 9:16)

Poor men have no voice…
If you are financially lacking, the marketplace will pay no attention to you. If you want a voice… if you want to be heard, having tangible wealth is one way for that to happen.

Opening blind eyes and raising the dead will do that too, so I don't want to pretend that money is the only way you get people's attention. It's just one way.

Why?

Because the world celebrates and pays attention to accomplishment, especially as it pertains to financial success. I'm not saying that it should be that way. I am simply stating the obvious… It is that way.

When I started selling copiers in Nashville in 1986, I wanted to excel for one big reason… I knew it would give me a platform and credibility with which I could share my testimony and bring others to Christ.

Being number one obviously meant more income for me, but I wanted influence. I wanted to be heard, and what I wanted people to hear was the love of God reaching into their heart, in the workplace.

By the end of my first year, I had set a record for the most copiers sold in a single year, and I was only in the territory less than eleven months. As a result, I was promoted to sales manager, bypassing others with much more experience, and replacing the current man in that position.

I had gained a platform.

In the next ten months, I led my team to experience a 430% year over year increase in sales. Oh yeah, in the process, I also led some of them to Christ. They saw my natural success and wanted whatever I had that made that possible. At least one of my sales reps not only got saved but went on to Bible school and into fulltime ministry!

It seems to me that Christians either shun money, seeing it as dirty and corrupting (which it can be) or they have fallen under the sway of the whole world and are chasing it like a dog on the beach chasing seagulls.

Solomon, the wealthiest man ever, said *"Will you set your eyes on that which is not? For* **riches certainly make themselves wings; They fly away like an eagle toward heaven.***"* (Proverbs 23:5) I think Solomon might have had a dog (-:

But there is a new breed of Christian arising. We've had some in every generation, who capture resources and with them subdue what is often called, the Seven Mountains of Influence (family, religion, education, media, entertainment, business, and government).

It's back to what Solomon said, *"money answers everything"*. You need money to feed your family or build a church. You need money to buy or shape education. You need money to have a media company or provide quality entertainment. Government needs money to run and godly leaders who know how to steward that money properly, honestly, and justly.

What some folks call the "mountain of business", I refer to as the "gates of commerce". Anyone can climb a mountain, but gates control entry to the city. He who controls the gates, controls the city. Solomon said, *"When the righteous are in authority, the people rejoice; But when a wicked man rules,* **the people groan**.*"* (Proverbs 29:2)

I've been hearing a lot of groaning since the overblown "pandemic" came to town and every government in the world simultaneously used the same talking points and followed the same protocols which in many cases were provably useless, even harmful, but were largely unchallenged until recently.

I say we need to quit groaning about the corruption and motivations that got us here. We need to get in positions of authority and lead our nations in righteousness.

Abram set the standard...
"Now when Abram heard that his brother was taken captive, **he armed his three hundred and eighteen TRAINED servants...***"* (Genesis 14:14) Abram didn't start the war, but he was sure to finish it. He didn't walk away licking his wounds and nursing his losses. He took action, engaged the enemy and recaptured what was stolen.

I contend that it's time that we did that... Recapture the gates that have been overrun. Use the resulting influence to take all the portals of influence!

But here's the tricky thing about war... It's a zero-sum game. We have to win it or be completely subjugated. That's the awful thing about war... You have to win it!

Look around the world at the subjugation that took place by heavy handed, even tyrannical leaders in nations we thought were bastions of freedom. Canada and Australia became China and North Korea in terms of their policies.

But it's not too late. We can and ultimately will take back the gates of commerce, because those gates don't belong to Hell... They're just temporarily occupied until men and women of God rise up, enter the fray and take back those gates!

Here are four things that we must address to take back the gates of commerce...

1. **Mindset:** Align your mind with God's Word. When He says, *"Be not afraid for the Lord your God is with you"*, (Numbers 14:9, Joshua 1:9, Deuteronomy 31:6, etc.) believe Him! Remember that *"greater is He that is in you, than he that is in the world"* (1 John 4:4) and give thanks to

God *"who always causes us to triumph"* (2 Corinthians 2:14) Develop a mindset of victory. Enlarge your vision. Expect great things! Bring every contradicting thought captive.

2. **Preparation:** *"Then there was war in the gates; Not a shield or spear was seen among forty thousand in Israel."* (Judges 5:8) As a nation, they were totally unprepared. Solomon said, *"For by wise counsel you will wage your own war."* (Proverbs 24:6)

We are responsible to wage our own war, and we do that with wise counsel. Whether it's your own personal war against lack, poverty, sickness, or lost relationships, generally speaking, you're going to have wage your own war. No one else is going to do it for you.

That takes planning and preparation. Jesus said, *"Or what king, going to make war against another king, does not sit down first and consider whether he is able with ten thousand to meet him who comes against him with twenty thousand?"* (Luke 14:31)

What's it going to take for you to take back the gates of commerce in your life? What's it going to take for you to be victorious in the gates of the city? Not so you can boast or stroke your ego, but so you can help protect the city, even the nation.

My friend Peter J. Daniels, had much success in the marketplace, amassing considerable wealth and using his position in the gates to influence his country. In 1971, a pornographic, LIVE stage-play with mixed sexes, nude on stage was coming to his city.

Peter used his considerable resources to muster media exposure and build public support to ban the show before it began. It went all the way to the Supreme Court and using his money as a defense for women being degraded and objectified, he succeeded in having the show kept out of the city.

3. **Strategy:** Mindset and preparation are very important but so is having a wise strategy. As Paul warns us in Ephesians 6:12 *"we do not war against flesh and blood"*, so we need the mind of Christ to have the right strategy.

   Some would suggest we just need to pray and fast. Others would suggest more aggression in some form. While I would never want to minimize prayer and fasting, I don't want to only rely on natural means by themselves.

   David said in Psalm 33:17, *"A horse is a vain hope for safety"*. What we need is Holy Spirit guided, natural actions. It's not either / or… It's both / and.

4. **Skill:** The thing about winning in business and life is that it is essential to train. When Abram's nephew Lot was kidnapped by a hostile force, he gathered up his 318 **trained** servants, and hunted the enemy down and recovered his nephew, along with all his goods and the women and people who were kidnapped with him.

   Think about this… How much property must you have to house 318 servants? How much money and provision must you have to carry their expenses day in and day out? Not to mention they would have had wives and children.

PLUS, he made sure his men were TRAINED! Don't expect to take territory and recapture the gates of commerce just because you want to. Invest in your mind. Invest in your skill development.

Become a highly trained servant of the Most Hight God and be prepared to go to the gates of commerce unashamedly and unwaveringly and unapologetically, compete successfully and regain control of what we have given up in the past. King David said, *"Praise be to the LORD my Rock, who TRAINS MY HANDS for war, my fingers for battle."* (PSALM 144:1)

The Promise
God made a promise to Abraham that his descendants would possess the gate of their enemies. (Genesis 22:17) and Paul reminds us that if we are in Christ, then WE ARE ABRAHAM'S SEED (Galatians 3:29).

But the gates are not going to be voluntarily handed over to us. It will be a struggle, a contest of will and wisdom, and spiritual authority. But remember Paul's word to us in 2 Corinthians 10:3… *"For though we walk in the flesh, we do not war according to the flesh."*

According to Paul, we do war. That's a given. Just don't war in a way that is dictated by the flesh. Moses warned, *"WHEN YOU GO TO WAR in your land against the enemy who oppresses you…"* (Numbers 10:9) It was never a matter of "IF", it's just a matter of WHEN.

Moses reminds us in Exodus 15:3 that, *"The **Lord is a man of war;** The Lord is His name."* In fact, fast forward to the end of the book (Revelation 19:11) … *"Now I saw heaven opened, and* *behold, a white horse. And He who sat on him was called Faithful and True, and in righteousness* **He judges and makes war.**"

So, my friend, I have a question for you…

ARE YOU READY?

By that I mean, are you ready to get equipped, enjoin the battle, and begin taking back the gates of commerce? If not you, who will fill the void? As you read through this book, I hope you will come away with more insight and revelation for succeeding in the gates.

If you want to walk with others on this same quest, be sure to check out MichaelPink.com/Secrets and join our amazing online mentoring and mentorship group.

CHAPTER 2

First Things First

"Seek first the kingdom of God and His righteousness,*
and all these things shall be added to you." (Jesus Christ)

A familiar Scripture to most, but what does it mean to you? How do you in a practical way, put this into practice? What does it look like? How does it shape your day?

I'll wait.

For most of my Christian walk, it simply meant that I would seek God and what was right by studying His Word and then going out with the new information and apprehending for myself whatever I could. And if I got in a jam, of course, I could always pray.

By the time I was 39, I had written several Scripture books including, <u>The Words in Red – The Teachings of Christ Compiled</u>, <u>Psalm 91 – The Ultimate Shield</u>, and perhaps most famously, <u>The Bible Incorporated – In Your Life, Job & Business</u>.

I thought I knew the Bible well and I loved teaching it. So, in 1994 we went to Guatemala to hold a Bible Incorporated Seminar at a big hotel. We were on a tight budget and hoping for a successful event, but three big things happened that greatly impacted our end result.

First of all, I had ordered 500 beautiful workbooks to be printed locally and delivered to the venue the morning of the event. The printer showed up with 5000 books, insisting that was what we ordered and demanded payment in full, or we couldn't have any workbooks.

Secondly, when we got inside the hotel, I was informed that the posters all over the city said, "Lunch Included", but were supposed to say, "Lunch NOT Included". With 250 attendees showing up at a world class hotel we either had to explain that it was a typo (and appear to not be keeping our word) or buy 250 people a nice catered lunch.

That was pricy!

Thirdly, as the day progressed, we offered the recording of the event for sale and our local team was to take payment and shipping info so we could mail them out. When the day was over, I was informed that virtually everyone in attendance bought.

I was so relieved! We put the cash box in a safe at the hotel and didn't even count it until after the weekend was over. As it turned out, the local team took no payments and got no shipping info. They considered it a sale when someone said they wanted the recording!

So, all in one day, we purchased 10 X the workbooks we needed, bought 250 people a nice lunch that wasn't in the budget, and generated zero sales at the back of the room.

It was a financial disaster and that doesn't include the team costs, travel, lodging, etc. Needless to say, at 39 years of age, I was a little shell shocked.

Simultaneous to all this was the fact that for the previous nine months, I had been unable to stand straight due to my back being out. I literally couldn't stand straight for a single moment in the day. And I was in frequent pain.

I sought the Lord concerning all of this and told Him that I didn't need a still small voice to whisper to me… I needed an unmistakable, undeniable response from him to confirm whether my destiny was in any way connected to Latin America.

I needed to know whether He still wanted me on the path of teaching His Word for work and business, and especially whether there was more to do in Central and South America.

So, I asked Him to heal my back and make me straight again if in fact He wanted me to continue. I honestly had zero expectation that I would be healed, as I had been prayed for many times in the past.

It was either the next day, or the one after that, when I got out of bed in our rented apartment in the diplomat section of Guatemala City that I suddenly noticed I was completely pain free, could move normally and was able to stand straight! I was completely healed and have remained healed ever since!

I asked Him what to do next and He directed me to do a few more seminars in the next three weeks but do them for free at local churches. We were invited to three churches including El Shaddai with Pastor Harold Caballeros and Verbo Church with Pastor Francisco Bianchi, where we gave folks a chance to freely give, and purchase the workbooks and full seminar on cassette if they wanted.

Between the three seminars, we had about 1,100 attendees, and we generated enough money to pay all our locally generated expenses for our approximately six weeks stay.

For me, it was the best of times and the worst of times. There were salvations, healings, and amazing encounters. I was asked by one presidential candidate to be his Minister of Finance if he won. God gave me favor in both the business and political realm, and I was leaving spiritually high, but financially drained.

By the time we got back home, there were two of every bill waiting for us at the post office. My credit line was maxed, as were my credit cards. I had no consulting work lined up, no clients to train lined up, and only one speaking engagement waiting for me which was at my own church, and I had told them before we left for Guatemala, that I didn't want an honorarium.

We had $300 in physical cash and no groceries in the house and a big stack of bills. I considered getting an early morning delivery job and perhaps one at night, which would leave me time in the day to rebuild my training and consulting business, which I had left behind because I thought I was going to spend the next year or longer in Central and South America.

My stress was palpable. How long was $300 going to last?

The next morning, I was shaving with a pit in my stomach and questions raging in my mind. What in the world was I going to do? What could I do?
That's when Jesus, in a perfectly calm voice, spoke to me in a clear and unmistakable way. He simply said, *"Pursue Me."*

I said, "Lord, I thought I had been pursuing you for many years now. In fact, I just did a seminar in Guatemala where I was teaching people Your ways. Doesn't that count as 'pursuing you'?"

I'm locked in a stare, looking in the mirror, waiting for more information. He spoke again… *"Pursue Me"*.

Tears began to well up in my eyes. I reasoned… "If You were a man in my backyard, I could go outside and chase after You, but I have no idea how to pursue You, if how I've lived my life thus far has not been that. Please…", I pleaded, "Give me a list of 10 things, 20 things, even 100 things to do, and I will do every one of them. Just tell me what I must do to pursue You."

Jesus spoke a third and final time saying in a firmness that made further questions unnecessary… *"PURSUE ME."*

Having no idea how to pursue an invisible God, I decided I would go in the living room and read my Bible, and pray, until…

Until He showed up in some way, so that His Word came to vibrant life in my soul, and I would remain in His Word until that Presence lifted.

On day one, as I prayed, God showed me something personal about the sin of Achan at the battle of Ai, where he coveted silver and gold which was supposed to be set aside for the Lord. Though I was a tither, I also had a case of the "covets", coveting the wealth of others, to the point of chasing riches instead of God.

At that moment, I was so worried about money that I was trying to figure out how to stretch out $300 for a few weeks by not paying bills, eating only macaroni and cheese, and pinching every penny! All the while, agonizing over what would happen when the last dollar was spent.

When I realized what was driving me, and what my mindset had been about money for quite some time, I repented and decided it would be better to find out right now what God would do.

No need for several weeks of suspense. So, we wired the entire $300 that day to a widow with a small child in Guatemala City, whose husband had been kidnapped and was presumed dead.

I then focused on pursuing God. But instead of pursuing His wisdom so I could be the rainmaker and make things happen, I pursued intimacy with Him and let Him fulfill the promise of "adding all these things". I spent hours with Him daily, took copious notes of what He spoke to me, and the strangest things began to happen.

The notion of 5 or 10 minutes of "quiet time" to start my day was completely out the window. I discovered that Jesus was always glad to see me and never in a hurry to leave. A short visit would be an hour, but typically, it would last 3 – 5 hours.

My mind was screaming, "I should be doing something!" but my spirit was having a party with the Word, and I didn't want it to end. Within a couple of days, God spoke to two different people and told them to give us money. (We hadn't had the chance yet to tell anyone about our predicament.)

We now had money for gas, food, and some small bills. Having no client work lined up, I just focused on pursuing Him in the mornings and going to the office in the afternoon.

Within a few days, I got a call from a friend in Canada who had no idea I had been out of the country. We hadn't spoken in about a year. He told me the Holy Spirit told him to call me and he wanted to know what was going on in my life.

I briefed him on the Guatemala trip and then he began to talk about a new magazine he was starting. He wanted some consulting from me and asked what I would charge to come up there for a week.

I told him if the Holy Spirit told him to call me, He could tell him how much to pay me. He prayed at the moment and then made a generous offer for me to come right away. In one week, I was completely caught up on my bills and living expenses and was chipping away at my debt.

We then set up a monthly retainer that covered all my needs going forward but was only part-time work. That's when I ran into a friend who, unbeknownst to me, had become VP of Business Development at the Christian television network known as INSP. He asked me if I would do an infomercial with my Biblical business training for the network and offered me a handsome royalty advance.

It was one thing after another coming my way without me doing anything but pursuing God. My publisher who had previously turned down my book ideas, contacted me to do a book and then another and another. All with nice royalty advances.

Before Guatemala, I couldn't get another book published, but suddenly, they were after me for book after book. Before I began pursuing God in this new way, it never occurred to me that I would have the opportunity to do an infomercial on a satellite network.

It just kept coming, month after month, year after year. That's when I learned that when I truly sought God's kingdom and righteousness first (aka pursued God), that He took responsibility for adding everything else to my life.

It was in my pursuit of Him, that He would guide me and tell me who to call and when. Pursuing Him was far more pleasurable than pursuing riches, which as Solomon said, *"make wings and fly way like an eagle toward heaven."* (Proverbs 23:5)

Stress was gone. Excitement was a daily experience. Life became so much fuller. Years later, I decided to study Matthew 6:33 again and amplify the text to its fullest meaning, using the original Greek and context as my source. Let this get inside you. Meditate on it. Let it change you...

"Make it your first priority with respect to your time, who or what you give honor to, even how you use your influence – the deliberate and purposeful directing of your thoughts and desires to seek, pursue and apprehend the rule, authority and dominion of God in your life, (including His counsels, interests and all things due Him). Include with that, the pursuit of His righteousness, integrity, virtue, purity of life, and correct way of thinking, feeling and acting. And any and all things that you need for life including your very food, drink and clothes will be added to you, laid beside you, annexed for you and given to you."

So let me encourage you my friend...

The best business advice I can give you in a snapshot is simply to "Pursue God". Marinate your mind in His Word. Let the Word speak. Ask the Holy Spirit to speak to you. Wait on Him. Listen. Write down what comes to you.

If you're new to this, you may wonder if it's just your thoughts or His. That's normal. Over time you will learn that He speaks to you from within your heart, not from outside your mind. His wisdom will rise up within you and you will have a certain "knowing". It will never contradict Scripture.

I would actually write out a Scripture long hand, and then write a response to Him about that Scripture as though I were sending him a personal letter. Then I would quiet myself, ask Him to speak to me, and I would listen. Often times, it was just a phrase or a word, but as I wrote down what I was sensing, it would oftentimes turn into a flow of wisdom and revelation that would change my life.

The Word of God (Jesus) and the Holy Spirit would literally teach me Scripture and give me profound understanding of things. You will never find a better counselor than Jesus. You will never find a better teacher than the Holy Spirit.

I have spent many years since then in pursuit of God, sometimes more than at other times. But in the process, He has shown me mysteries from His Word and revealed secrets to me from His creation. In the remainder of this book, I will continue passing on to you what took me years to acquire.

Once you have learned to pursue God and actually connect with Him through His Word and by His Spirit, you are then ready to… walk with Him. That's what the next chapter is about, and it's a real GAME CHANGER!

CHAPTER 3

Walk With God – A Game-Changing Strategy

*"Enoch **walked with God**; and he was not,
for God took him."* (Genesis 5:24)

*"And what does the Lord require of you, but to do justly, to love mercy,
and to **walk humbly with your God**?"* (Micah 6:8)

*"For **as many as are led** by the Spirit of God,
these are sons of God."* (Romans 8:14)

Have you ever gone on a hike through the woods or into the mountains with a friend? Or maybe just a long walk on a deserted beach?

Chances are that your conversation was sporadic. Sometimes talking. Sometimes just taking in the beauty of the moment. But regardless of the level of conversation, you were in fact walking with them and hopefully enjoying their company.

If you had a question about anything, you could ask them. If you had a thought you wanted to share, you were free to do so. You were walking with them, and the lines of communication were open, even if there were extended periods of silence.

So it is with the Lord – if you will allow it. You can go through your day conscious of His Presence and occasionally asking Him about things, telling Him things, and making your requests known.

When I was in sales, and later as a trainer for corporations, when I would go on calls with their sales teams, I would pray before going in. I would often ask the Lord things like, "Show me the kingdom men and women who are looking for the King but haven't found Him yet. I want to introduce them to You."

Inevitably during the course of the day, it would often become apparent who God was working on. It was usually the rough around the edges person, who if anything, seemed crude and not ready to surrender their life to God.

On one such occasion, as one of my team members and I were heading into a corporation to do a final day of training, we stopped in the parking lot to pray.

As I was praying but not feeling particularly spiritual, something amazing happened. (In all honesty, that prayer felt more like a duty than an inspired moment.) But that's when God played what I call, "a video clip" for me. Some might call it a vision, but it doesn't matter.

What I saw was Heaven opened up, and someone (I believe it was an angel) with a bow and arrow in hand. And they released that arrow with great resolve, striking a man in my client's office in the heart. The man it struck was a charming fellow, but one of the most fluent in the use of four-letter words I had ever seen. He was very funny, but he was lost as a goose in a Canadian snowstorm.

And I knew the arrow was a message. And I knew what the message was. And I knew I was the one who was supposed to give him the message. Remember, we weren't at church. This was an industrial service company. I wasn't contracted to bring

God messages to their employees. I was there to provide sales training.

But it was an arrow, and I was given the privilege of delivering it. Would I leave that arrow in my quiver because it was not politically correct to release an arrow of the gospel, or would I draw back my bow and shoot him at point blank range?

Of course, I shot him!

I don't want to die with the beautiful arrows God has given me, still in their quiver. (Oh God, please give me more arrows to shoot!)

It was the end of the day before I had the chance to speak to Shane (not his real name). I was preparing to leave and catch my flight back home and I was running late, when I ran into Shane in the hallway and realized I still had the arrow in my quiver.

So, I released it. At point blank range.

I told Shane about the "video clip" I had seen in the parking lot and that he was in that video. I told him that God was releasing an arrow straight into his heart and the arrow was a message from the Father and the message was… *"The Father is calling you back to Himself."*

He literally grabbed me by the lapel of my suit and pulled me into his office and with ashen face said, "Tell me more!"

So, I did.

And he wept.

And he was born again. The arrow hit its mark! The old man was dead, and a new creation stood before me, wiping away his tears.

Sometimes walking with God means hearing what He is saying (or seeing what He is showing) and then obeying Him. Not too complicated really, and very rewarding.

But sometimes it's all about business.

I was out doing a training call with a new salesman at a company who sold CNC (Computerized Numerical Control) manufacturing equipment. When we arrived at one of his calls, the owner came out to inform us that he had just purchased from the competition the day before and had taken delivery, claiming it was $15,000 less for the "very same thing".

The salesman turned around to walk out the door realizing we were too late, but I asked if we could see the equipment he had purchased in operation.

The owner was only too glad to show off his new $53,000 investment. While speaking with him and learning about his business, the Holy Spirit spoke to me completely out of the blue. He told me we were going to walk out with the sale for my client's equipment which represented a $68,000 investment.

That seemed so crazy to me that I literally laughed out loud in the middle of a serious business conversation. Needless to say, they thought I was a bit strange, but I couldn't tell anyone what the Holy Spirit had just revealed.

But because I was walking with Him and listening to Him, I continued the conversation with the prospect, and by using the Moses Questioning Strategy, (Book 2, chapter 1) uncovered the necessary information that led to him concluding that he had made a terrible mistake buying from the competitor.

POWER PRINCIPLE: **Selling is not about telling. It's about listening, so learn to ask the right questions and the sale becomes much, much easier.**

The end result was that he returned the equipment he had just purchased and bought from my client instead. That day we walked out with a signed agreement and a check. That would never have happened if I wasn't walking with God.

It's not really a big mystery. There's no woo woo about it. You just do like Paul said in Ephesians 6… "praying always". For me that is simply asking the Lord as I walk through my day if there is something He wants me to say, hear or see, or perhaps there's someplace He wants me to go or something particular to do.

I have found when I take His detour and do what He asks, even when it completely disrupts my plans, my schedule and time sensitive tasks, He has a way of making up for it.

I was flying back to Nashville from the West Coast and was looking forward to the long flight because it gave me several hours of non-interrupted time for working on a proposal I wanted to get done.

I was seated in an aisle seat at the bulkhead which was ideal for leg room and minimal interruptions. A man in his thirties and his mother in her sixties took the two seats to my immediate left. I had hoped for more elbow room but opened my laptop and began working before they had even closed the door to the plane.

I was sending a nonverbal message to the passengers next to me, that I wanted to be left to my work. But as I was walking with the Lord while sitting in my seat, He said something to me about talking to them about being "born again".

I hate to admit this, but I was so focused on my business agenda and self-imposed time pressures, that I literally turned around and looked at all the passengers filling the plane behind me and told the Lord, they looked like they all needed to be born again. I then resumed my work, ignoring what He had just spoken to me.

The man next to me turned and asked if I was working. I thought to myself, "What does it look like?" I curtly replied, "Yes."
He then asked me what kind of work I did. I told him I taught Biblical principles and strategies for sales and business, hoping that short sentence would end the conversation.

It did not.

He then asked me, "Are you what they call, a born again Christian?"

"Yes", I replied.

Then he asked me, "What does it mean to be born again?"

I guess my level of disobedience had its limits. I closed my computer and for the rest of the long flight, he and his mother eagerly asked me about my faith. They were hungry to know more. Someone had obviously planted the seed. I merely watered that time, and trusted God to bring the increase. (1 Corinthians 3:6)

Although I was in the end, happy to be a witness, I was also disappointed that I got no work done towards future client acquisition.

When I got off the plane, my wife handed me a letter that had come in from a Fortune 100 company, with whom I had no previous contact. They invited me to come and speak to their mid-level managers at corporate headquarters in New Jersey.

That was an account I would never have even had on my prospect list, let alone expect to secure, and here it was, handed to me on a platter when my flight touched down. I did absolutely nothing to get that account. It was just given to me.

Thus, I began to learn that walking with God and doing what He asks is in fact the shortest path to success, even when it looks like a detour. However, the key is to not make up your own detours, but rather be on the lookout for His invitations and take them.

I could literally fill the rest of this book with examples of doing just that. Walking with God in such a way as to hear Him or perhaps see something He wants me to see, and then acting on it.

It's like walking with a close friend all day. Not always talking, but always being ready to listen. And then not ignoring His unmistakable voice, but drinking it in and communing with Him, and following through on what He says. Many, many times, it's just great conversation where I am learning something profound.

Didn't Jesus say that He didn't speak on His own authority but the Father who sent Him gave Him a command what He should say and speak?

Walking with God is such a strategic advantage in the marketplace. The paths He will take you on result in the kind of stories you will want to tell your grandchildren about.

Sometimes they are so specific and have an urgency to them, that if you don't act on right away, you'll miss the opportunity. I have a profound chapter about another game changing reality about the "eth" of God, which is really about timing. But for now, let me give you an example…

I was in my office at home, when out of the blue, the Holy Spirit quickened to me that I needed to immediately stop what I was doing and call a particular CEO who headed up a Christian CEO ministry that I wanted to make inroads with.

People had been suggesting for years that I reach out to him, but I was really waiting for God's timing. When it came, the CEO who had never heard of me, took my call and we quickly discovered we were both going to be traveling to Atlanta the next week.

I asked him to speak at my Selling Among Wolves conference that was scheduled there the next week and he asked me to speak at their annual convention in Jamaica and other cities over the next few years.

That opened a flood of opportunities that resulted in new business opportunities for me and many more folks coming to know Jesus.

I believe that God is very interested in helping you succeed in business, but I have noticed He is also interested in advancing His kingdom and taking territory back from the sway of the devil. Here's one incredible example…

I was invited by an international life insurance company to train their sales teams in two different countries, a few days apart. I was known as a Christian sales trainer who taught Biblical wisdom for succeeding in sales, but I was instructed to not make any overt references to Scripture.

Before arriving there however, the Lord told me of His plan, that He wanted me to start a fire in those countries. Not sure exactly what that meant, I traveled there and shared with the company president what I felt God had given me to do.

He was a Christian and told me that out of the 45 sales reps in the next day's training, only about 15 were actually believers. I asked if it would be alright, if at the end of the training, I could give an invitation for folks to receive Christ.

He replied hesitatingly in the affirmative, as neither one of us had ever seen or done an invitation to receive Christ in a corporate sales training setting.

At the end of the day of training, I shared an amazing illustration about how God wanted to take up residence in them and let them know I would pray with any of them that wanted to invite God to live in them.

The president closed out the meeting by reminding everyone when and where to turn in their expense receipts and what time the Monday sales meeting would start, etc. He then added, *"If anyone wants Michael to pray with them, he will be over here at the side of the room."*

Not exactly "with every head bowed and every eye closed" with "Just As I Am" playing softly on the piano. But apparently God doesn't have to have a church setting to accomplish what He wants.

I don't think either of us expected what happened next…

The entire room of 45 salespeople stood up as one person and came to the front to receive prayer and invite the Lord to live in them. As I prayed with them individually, the president sat on the front row, with tears streaming down his face. His entire sales team dedicated their life to God!

Even the video contractor who recorded the meeting asked if he could come forward for prayer. I had never seen anything like it before, especially in a corporate setting.

That scene would repeat itself a couple days later when we got to the next country. Somehow, God used that simple illustration to settle in their hearts the reality of God and their need, indeed their secret desire, to be cleansed and receive the indwelling presence of the Holy Spirit.

So, remember my friend, walking with God is a two-way street. It's not all about your business. God is mindful of that and desires to meet all of your needs. After preaching from Peter's boat, Jesus told Peter to throw his nets back in the water and God literally filled his boat!

But just like he did with Peter, he will also ask you to be His voice on the earth, in the context of your business dealings, and to extend the love and kindness of God to a world that desperately needs Him.

Will you say "yes" to the Lord?

I have led only one person to the Lord in a church, but many, many more on the highways and byways of the world of commerce. And not one of them was planning to be in church to hear the gospel.

We are called to be His ambassadors (2 Corinthians 5:20). We have been purchased with the very blood of Christ (Acts 20:28)

In fact, Paul tells us in 1 Corinthians 6:19 & 20... *"Do you not know that your body is the temple of the Holy Spirit who is in you, whom you have from God, and **you are not your own**? For **you were bought at a price**; therefore glorify God in your body and in your spirit, which are God's."*

In Daniel 2:28 we learn *"There is a God in heaven who reveals secrets."* But to whom does He reveal them? Psalm 25:14 says, *"The secret of the Lord is with those who fear Him."* And Solomon, the wisest man who ever lived said that God's *"secret counsel is with the upright"*. (Proverbs 3:32)

God has secrets He wants to share with you. Are you willing to pursue Him and walk with Him to learn what He has to share? I have found that when I pay attention to His business, He takes care of mine.

That isn't to say that we're neglectful of our business or slothful in its execution. Au contraire. Like Paul said when asked about the grace of God, *"Shall we continue in sin that grace may abound? Certainly not!"* (Romans 6:1-2) Neither should we be slothful about business that His provision should abound.

It really comes down to doing the one thing, the right thing, at the right time. And that my friend, is easiest to do when you are tuned into His Word and His Spirit. Paul called this having *"the mind of Christ."* (1 Corinthians 2:16)

Walk with God.

It is your right and your privilege.

It is also your strategic advantage.

CHAPTER 4

The Bible: God's Instruction Book for Life and Business

*"So shall My word be that goes forth from My mouth; It **shall not return to Me void**, But it **shall accomplish** what I please, **And it shall prosper** in the thing for which I sent it."* (Isaiah 55:11)

***"He who despises the word will be destroyed**,*
But he who fears the commandment will be rewarded." (Proverbs 13:13)

*"For you have **magnified Your Word above all Your name**."* (Psalm 138:2)

Here's the deal… Too many Christians try to live a compartmentalized life. They put God first and family second. From there they figure out where to put friends, fitness, and financial matters, etc.

At least that's the theory.

But how does one put God first? Is it a measurement of time? Is it defined by your financial contributions? Is it the accumulation of good works or personal sacrifice?

I would contend that there's a better way to structure your life and it looks a lot more like a wagon wheel with God as the hub from which everything flows, rather than an org chart where He is relegated to a compartment or time slot.

Would you really like to know Jesus better? Would you like to know what He thinks, how He thinks and what is important to Him? Would you like to know what He knows about things like work and business?

Men like Johannes Kepler (who formulated three major laws of planetary motion which enabled Isaac Newton to devise the law of gravitation) and Matthew Maury known as the Pathfinder of the Seas, for discovering the actual paths in the oceans that enabled ships to travel faster once they learned to go with the currents, both got their inspiration for their scientific discoveries from God's Word.

People thought it strange and even foolish to look to Scripture for scientific insights, to which Matthew Maury wrote, *"I have been blamed by men of science, both in this country and in England, for quoting the Bible in confirmation of the doctrines of physical geography. The Bible, they say, was not written for scientific purposes, and is therefore no authority in matters of science. I beg pardon! The Bible IS authority for everything it touches."*

I contend that the same is true for business. Do you want success?

In Joshua 1:8, God's Word actually promises success in life … *"This **Book of the Law** (instruction) shall not depart from your mouth, but you shall meditate in it day and night, that you may observe to do according to all that is written in it. For **then YOU WILL MAKE YOUR WAY prosperous**, and then **you will have <u>GOOD SUCCESS</u>**."*

In Psalms 1 we read *"Blessed is the man who <u>walks not in the counsel of the ungodly</u>, nor stands in the path of sinners, nor sits in the seat of the scornful; But **his delight is in the <u>law (instruction)</u> of the Lord**, And in His (instruction) law he meditates day and night. He shall be like a tree planted by the rivers of water, that brings forth its fruit in its season, whose leaf also shall not wither;* **and whatever he does shall prosper.***"*

People think of the Word of God like it's a dusty collection of religious words cobbled together by men of old that have little relevance to today except possibly as a mild inspiration or sentiments to be read at funerals.

Let me be brilliantly clear on this… The Word of God is a person. His name is Jesus Christ. The apostle John wrote this about Jesus… *"In the beginning was the Word, and the Word was with God,* **and the Word was God***. He was in the beginning with God. All things were made through Him, and without Him nothing was made that was made. In Him was life, and the life was the light of men."*

As my wife Judy says, "You can't separate God from His Word."

Yet too many people try to find their way through life with the Word as an afterthought. They don't find it relevant. They don't connect with it. They read a chapter and got nothing from it.

Well guess what? That's normal. Everyone experiences that. Don't feel bad. And don't quit! Push through. God said in Jeremiah 23:29, *"Is not my Word like a hammer that breaks the rock in pieces?"*

In Matthew 4:4, Jesus said, "Man *shall not live by bread alone, but by every word that proceeds from the mouth of God."* And in John 6:63, He said that the flesh profits NOTHING, but the words He speaks are spirit and life!

Yet people persist in trying to do things in their fleshly strength and wisdom. Why? Because we have an enemy who comes to take away the seed of His Word, the moment it lands on your heart, rendering it seemingly impotent and by extension, worthless. Mark 4:15.

As a result, people who don't choose to pursue God and know Him, treat His Word as optional at best, irrelevant and fictional at worst. But look at Proverbs 13:13… *"He who despises the word will be destroyed, But he who fears the commandment will be rewarded."*

The word translated as "despises" also means to "hold as insignificant". The word translated as "destroyed" also means to bind. You could say that *"folks who hold God's Word as insignificant will find themselves in a bind."*

You may be thinking that God's Word is significant and very important, but you have found very little in Scripture that is practical to the rough and tumble competitive world of sales and business building. So let me help you out on that…

The historical Jewish view of Scripture sees God's Word on four levels. The first is called the "p'shat" where you interpret Scripture at its surface, face value meaning. When Scripture says, *"Do not commit adultery",* it literally means "Do not commit adultery". (Exodus 20:14)

When it comes to business there are a number of passages that on a surface level speak to common business practices. For example, Proverbs 27:23 says, *"Be diligent to know the state of your flocks, And attend to your herds;"* That's pretty straight forward and helpful, but there's not a lot of direct discussion about marketplace practices in the whole of Scripture.

The next level in Jewish interpretation of Scripture is called "remez" which is the allegorical interpretation, (the meaning beyond just the literal sense.) An example would be a story that teaches a practical lesson like comparing the man who built his house on the rock to the man who built upon the sand. It's not intended to be taken literally, but rather to teach a very important lesson.

Think of a remez is a hint to a broader context that relies on your ability to, by association, connect the dots between written or spoken words and concepts. It contains a hidden message, or a deeper meaning, thought to be a treasure just below the surface or hidden behind the words themselves.

A remez is like a clue to a deeper mystery. If you were trying to figure out a mystery that a friend knew the answer to, you might say, "Give me a remez" which is to say, "Give me a clue."

Jesus tells the story of a man who found a hidden treasure in a field, then sold everything so he could buy it. He gave another similar story in which a merchant found one pearl of great price and sold everything to obtain it. Neither story was meant to be taken literal. Both stories were speaking about the kingdom of God being the thing worth selling everything for, in order to have.

But now, take it over to business…

These stories can really speak to the power of focus. What is the ONE THING that you are willing to trade your life for?

Think about that!

Would you agree that life is precious?

Everything you see and hear on earth loses meaning for you if you don't have life. Life is the most precious gift imaginable, yet every day, so many people trade the most precious thing they have (their very life) for lesser gods and lesser goals.

It's as if their life has no value, no meaning, no worth, no direction.

Make no mistake; **you are trading your life for something**. Why not trade it for something great?!?! Why settle for low living and mediocre goals when we were designed and built for so much more?

You know what your problem is? You haven't identified what dominant goal you are willing to trade your life for and secondly, you have no idea how to make it happen.

Maybe you're content to trade your life for "just getting by", but that doesn't work for me. I suspect that doesn't work for you either or you wouldn't be reading this book.

Do YOU KNOW what you are willing to trade your life for? As Curly said in the 1991 film, City Slickers, "It's just one thing". Everything else is subordinate to it.

Like Jesus, you will "set your face like a flint" towards that one thing. Nothing will make you abandon that course. But when you don't know what that one thing is, every path seems right.

I had a telemarketing call left on my voice mail recently. They promised we could make thousands of dollars a week from home, without selling and with very little effort.

I wonder how many suckers fell for that one. My wife Judy wisely said, "Even if it was 100% legitimate, it has nothing to do with our life." She's right!

You see, we have a course, and we are set upon it, but when you don't know the course, the goal, the dream, then every promise looks good.

The number one reason people accomplish little in life while desiring many things is because they haven't figured out what that one thing is and therefore haven't set their face like flint towards accomplishing that one thing.

Maybe you had it at one time but lost it. I have a word for you… GET IT BACK!

Don't let the devil hold on to stolen property, including stolen dreams. The number one way he is able to hold on to your dreams is by handing you excuses that you accept. Only when excuses become unacceptable, will you find the resolve to take back what was stolen from you!

I could go on about this, but I get that and a lot more from those two stories Jesus told which were meant to convey a different meaning. If you want to take your life to the next level, learn how to see and understand the remez level of Biblical interpretation.

The third level of interpretation is called the d'rash. The term comes from the process of threshing grain – separating the wheat from the chaff.

Whereas remez is more allegorical, d'rash deals with parables or riddles, which can be far more difficult to understand. It's considered the mystery or enigmatic level and may include the use of gematria (otherwise known as numerical Bible codes) to connect Scriptures that would be otherwise unrelated.

A classic example of a Biblical riddle is found in Revelation 13:18… *"Here is wisdom. Let him who has understanding calculate the number of the beast, for it is the number of a man: His number is 666."* To understand this Scripture, you're going to have to go deep, look for cross references in Scripture and historical usage. While it may very well have a literal fulfillment such as the total numeric value of the letters of the beast's name, it clearly holds a much more profound and weighty meaning.

Consider Ecclesiastes 1:9… *"That which has been, is what will be, That which is done is what will be done, And there is nothing new under the sun."* There is a mystery to this verse, a deep but practical meaning that wise investors have used to their benefit.

It's about cycles.

W.D. Gann, (1878 – 1955) is perhaps the most mysterious and most successful stock and commodity traders who ever lived. He often quoted this passage in Ecclesiastes and said, "To make a success you must continue to study past records because the market in the future will be a repetition of the past.

If I have the data, I can tell by the study of cycles when a certain event will occur in the future. The limit of future predictions based on exact mathematical law is only restricted by lack of knowledge of correct data on past history to work from."

My great grandfather James Stewart understood the relationship between cycles and commodity prices and used that knowledge to his great profit. One day in the 1920's he took his grandson (my father) out to lunch in Toronto where his office was.

When they returned from lunch, he checked his account and noted that he had made $85,000 while away at lunch. That would be about $1.4 million in today's currency! He actually came closer to any man in history to actually cornering the wheat market by practically applying this principle found in Ecclesiastes.

Finally, there is the "sod" level of Biblical interpretation. It's considered the spiritual or "secret" level of understanding, which the Lord is happy to reveal to those who walk in the fear of the Lord. (Psalm 25:15)

When I study the Tabernacle of Moses, I find a ton of "sod". The spiritual revelation combined with the practical application of the 7 pieces of "furniture" and the three "levels" are for me, the most profound and practical revelation of Scripture for business. As you progress through this book, you will learn many of them that will literally rock your world!

In closing, I believe the Apostle Paul was familiar with these four levels of interpretation and referred to them in Ephesians 3:18 when he said, *"That you may be able to comprehend with all saints what is the **breadth**, and **length**, and **depth**, and **height**…"* (Ephesians 3:18)

As you journey through this book with me, I will attempt to demonstrate by example and with teaching, the efficacy of God's Word and the highly practical relevance to the realm most people spend a great deal of time in – the marketplace, be that their job or business.

Perhaps the reason folks haven't seen the Word as an incredible business tutor, is because besides not simply reading and meditating up on it, they never understood its various levels and how profoundly they speak to everyday marketplace issues.

From this day forward, that need never be your story. In fact, I hope to hear from you either through our online community mentorship site or simply by email, the things God has shown you to apply to business.

If you can stand on my shoulders and go further than I, then I have done my job and I will rejoice with you!

CHAPTER 5

Thinking The Thoughts of God
(Accessing God's Wisdom on Demand)

*"**I will give you words and wisdom** that none of your adversaries will be able to resist or contradict."* (Luke 21:15)

*"**Let this mind be in you**, which was also in Christ Jesus"* (Phil. 2:5)

*"But **we have the mind of Christ.**"* (1 Corinthians 2:16)

I have consulted businesses across a wide spectrum and the most common question I'm asked before being asked to consult for them is "Have you ever worked in our industry before?"

I've consulted in the technology sector, the printing industry, industrial manufacturing, clothing producers, financial sector, real estate and more. It's always the same thing at the beginning… "What do you know about our specialty or niche?"

And with few exceptions, I usually had no experience or body of knowledge in the field I was being asked to work in. And yet, in every case, the client got so much more than they ever dreamed possible.

How was that possible?

It's simple really. So simple that most Christians miss it. We have the mind of Christ. Meaning, that we can access His wisdom and know what to do. In fact, and surprisingly so, this is not just a New Testament promise. Look at what Solomon said in Proverbs 3:5-6…

> *"Trust in the Lord with all of your heart.*
> *And lean not on your own understanding.*
> *In all your ways acknowledge Him*
> *And He will direct your paths."*

But I want to draw your attention to the word, "acknowledge" in this passage. It's the Hebrew word, "yada", and it implies much more than a casual knowing. In fact, it is the exact same word used in Genesis 4:1, *"And Adam **knew** Eve his wife, and she conceived."*

I used to think that acknowledging God was similar to tipping your hat to Him in respect when you walked in a room, or like so many college football players after a big win, want to *"acknowledge their Lord and Savior Jesus Christ."*

In point of fact, the act of acknowledging God, speaks of an intimate, deep and personal connection with Him. That verse could read, *"In all your ways be intimately connected in close fellowship with Him, and He will direct your paths."*

That makes sense. If you're walking in fellowship with Him, you will much more likely follow His leading and be directed in all your paths.

Up until recently, I looked at having the mind of Christ as being the result of a set aside time of seeking the Lord on a matter. While that certainly is a good practice bearing good fruit, there is something I overlooked in the past.

It is the fact that on many, many occasions in business and life, I was operating in the wisdom and mind of Christ at an unconscious level. It felt intuitive to me. I had the answers to complex issues for which I had no previous training or background in. This is and was a regular occurrence.

But isn't that along the same lines as when Jesus warned, *"You will be brought before kings and rulers for My name's sake…Settle it therefore in your minds **not to meditate beforehand how to answer**, for **I will give you a mouth and wisdom**, which none of your adversaries will be able to withstand or contradict."* (Luke 21:12, 14-15)

Jesus was letting us know that in times of coming persecution that there would be no need to think through our response when hauled in for questioning. At the very moment we needed it, we would have the wisdom and the words.

Well, guess what?

The same is true for business. It's how I ran my consulting practice. Take for example a large midwestern hydraulic equipment manufacturer with facilities in two states. On any given day the number of "late orders" that were still in the manufacturing business beyond the promised ship date was over 100.

It had been that way for more than a decade.

They had previously brought in manufacturing experts, one of which was considered the touchstone of manufacturing process wisdom. Despite significant investment in process improvement, nothing moved the needle.

It was more an act of desperation when the president asked if I thought I could help solve the problem. Despite having no manufacturing experience, I replied in the affirmative.

I was sent to their facility in the South to do a one-day training of the supervisors with the hope that maybe something I taught them could bring some improvement. No one was optimistic, but I had the mind of Christ.

The training that I came up with for how they could manage their teams better, resulted in an approximately 80% reduction in late orders the very next week. The following week, there late orders were down to single digits.

The president was stunned. They hadn't seen that level of efficiency and "on time" orders for at least fifteen years. And it was accomplished immediately, after just one day of training from a non-expert with no manufacturing experience.

But here's the thing… At the time, I didn't realize I was operating in the mind of Christ. I didn't think of it quite in those terms. I realized I had no clue how to solve their problem in a manufacturing facility employing hundreds of people, so I went with Proverbs 3:5-6.

The net result was I had His mind and His wisdom for the situation, and I infused it into the skeptical plant supervisors and the result was as dramatic as it was quick.

Another example…
A man called me from a tech company in Texas. He was in dire straits. His business was on the verge of collapsing and he had heard of me through the radio.

"Do you have any experience in battery conservation technologies?" came the question. "What's that?" came my reply.

But just like the manufacturing facility, I knew the problems were most likely with the people and if we could rearrange their mindset, we could most likely change their outcome.

He then proceeded to explain his business and the depth of problems he had and asked if I thought I could help him. I was his last hope and the money he would have to pay for me to come was his last.

It seemed like a big gamble. But it wasn't really.

I asked him a very penetrating series of questions… I asked if he was married and had kids, and I was informed that not only that, but he had a couple of adorable, very young grand kids.

I then asked if they were taken hostage and the ransom was that he had to turn the business around in 90 days or he would never see his grandkids alive again, would he start planning their funeral or would he turn the business around?

When he responded that unquestionably, he would turn the business around, then I informed him, that I could help, and we would make that happen. I flew out and spent three days with him and his team, giving them the insights, I was getting from accessing the mind of Christ, and then I flew home.

It was probably a couple years or so later when I heard back from him. He called to let me know how much I had helped him and to thank me for helping him turn it around. He let me know that he had just sold the company for a big fat payoff and was moving to Florida to comfortably retire.

The couple examples I shared with you were not the exception. They were the norm. Not because I was or am "super spiritual", but rather because I was aware of how technically unqualified I was in all the industries I worked in.

I knew how much I needed, valued, and ultimately embraced what God would show me in the course of stepping out and into their worlds with a confident expectation that He would indeed direct my paths and give me His wisdom.

Thinking the thoughts of God is not the privilege of a highly vetted few. They are offered to any and all who want to walk in intimate relationship with Him. This privilege is truly a game changing strategy!

CHAPTER 6

How To Defeat the Giants in Your Life
(12 Lessons from David's Victory Over Goliath)

*"Therefore, David ran **and stood over (Goliath),** took his sword and drew it out of its sheath **and killed him,** and cut off his head with it."* (1 Samuel 17:51)

*"These four were born to the giant in Gath and **fell by the hand of David** and by the hand of his servants."* (2 Samuel 21:22)

*"I have found David the son of Jesse, **a man after mine own heart**, which shall fulfil all my will."* (Acts 13:22)

Goliath is a type or picture of any demonic or ungodly resistance standing between you and your destiny in God. When David contended with Goliath, his approach and the strategy he modeled, will help anyone overcome any adversary or adversity in life.

1) IT STARTS WITH ATTITUDE
*"And David left his supplies in the hand of the supply keeper, **ran to the army**, and came and greeted his brothers."* (1 Samuel 17:22)
David knew that his brothers were with the troops on the front lines across from the Philistines, but he was the youngest of eight and was expected to look after the sheep.

One day David's father Jesse, told him to take bread and cheese to the troops and see how his brothers were doing. David was eager to do so, leaving early the next morning for the front lines. After dropping off the food he took that occasion to run to the army and greet his brothers. He was excited to be there!

David didn't gripe about having to take care of the sheep. He didn't complain about having to make a supply run for his brothers. He was eager to help. In short, he had a great attitude.

What is attitude? One day, I was writing by a lake in Tennessee, and I wanted a good definition for "attitude". Not having my computer or a dictionary with me, I asked the Lord to give me one. This is what I wrote down…

> **Attitude:** "A deep seated, chosen belief, either positive or negative, that sets in motion corresponding behavior, generally resulting in a self-fulfilling prophecy."

Attitude is the raw energy motivating every successful sales professional and entrepreneur. Without motivation, nothing moves, skills deteriorate, strategies gather dust and principles have nothing to empower.

It has to do with what you believe about things. What do you believe about your customers? What do you believe about you? About your chances of success? About your strengths and weaknesses? Have you overestimated your weaknesses and underestimated your strengths or the other way around?

What do you believe about your potential, about the opportunities and challenges that lay ahead? What do you believe about your profession or industry?

What do you believe about God? About His love for you? About His generosity towards you? About His desire to teach you, encourage you, bless you, etc.?

We don't know a lot about David's youth, but we can see that he had a great outlook on life and was eager to be where the action was. David didn't hesitate to run to the front lines. He was ready to serve in any way he could.

It's been said that attitude determines altitude and to a very large extent, that is true.

2) RECOGNIZE THE PROBLEM
"Then as he talked with them, there was the champion, the Philistine of Gath, Goliath by name, coming up from the armies of the Philistines; and he spoke according to the same words. So David heard them. And all the men of Israel, when they saw the man, fled from him and **were dreadfully afraid."** (1 Samuel 17:23-24) Until you recognize the problem, you can't fix it. Many of us, turn a blind eye to problems, hoping they will go away, but they seldom do.

David saw Goliath which everyone thought was the problem, but Goliath wasn't the problem, and he would soon prove that. The problem was that no one had the courage to fight Goliath. They were all in fear.

David recognized that Goliath wasn't just defying Israel, he was defying God. All that was needed was someone to come in the name of the Lord of Hosts and God would deliver them. God was looking for a champion and until David showed up, there wasn't one. David had the heart of a champion and God delivered him.

Don't attack the symptom of the problem. Attack the root of the problem. Goliath wasn't too big to defeat. Israel had a history of defeating giants in Joshua's day. The problem was fear and the root of that was unbelief.

David believed God. He knew that Israel was a covenant nation with God and God would deliver. In fact, he pointed out that Goliath was not part of the covenant when he asked, *"Who is this **uncircumcised** Philistine, that he should defy the armies of the living God?"* (1 Samuel 17:26) In other words David was saying, "Hey guys… Goliath is not circumcised. He is not in covenant with God. We are. We got this!"

3) VERIFIES THE REWARD
"What shall be done for the man who kills this Philistine and takes away the reproach from Israel?" (1 Samuel 17:26) David was merely confirming what he had already been told… *"It shall be that the man who kills him the king will enrich with great riches, will give him his daughter, and give his father's house exemption from taxes in Israel."* (1 Samuel 17:25)

Being mindful of the reward for success can be a strong motivating factor. Set goals for yourself with rewards for achievement. I believe David was motivated by the reward, as he confirmed it twice after hearing it the first time. If it didn't matter to him, he wouldn't have double verified.

Use rewards for self-motivation. For example, if you lose a certain amount of weight, you might want to reward yourself with a new wardrobe. If you hit a certain sales target or business objective, perhaps you'll reward yourself and the family with a vacation of some kind.

When challenged, by his brothers who were obviously threatened by David's boldness, he responds with two questions… *"What have I done now? Is there not a cause?"* (1 Samuel 17:29)

His words were heard and reported to King Saul. When you make a bold stand, it will be noticed. Don't be surprised where that may take you.

When David was brought before Saul he said, *"Let **no man's heart fail** because of him; your servant will go and fight with this Philistine."* (1 Samuel 17:32) He addresses their pain point (their hearts were in deep fear) and volunteered to fight. When his qualifications were challenged in the job interview with Saul, notice how he replied…

4) POSITIONING
David positioned himself **as a warrior** and a **former guardian** of his father's sheep… *"Your servant **used to** keep his father's sheep."* (1 Samuel 17:34) David didn't say that he was a skilled shepherd. He put that in the past and positioned himself in the eyes of Saul as a warrior.

David gives a double witness of his previous success to cement the perception that he wanted to portray, that he was a ready and able warrior… *"and when a lion or a bear came and took a lamb out of the flock, I went out after it and struck it, and delivered the lamb from its mouth; and when it arose against me, I caught it by its beard, and struck and killed it."* (1 Samuel 17:34-35)

David then summarizes his success in a single sentence and points to the only logical conclusion Saul could arrive at. *"Your servant has killed both lion and bear; and this uncircumcised Philistine will be like one of them…"* (1 Samuel 17:36) He used the power of "story" to appeal to the heart and then used logic to satisfy the mind. The sale was made, and Saul said, *"Go, and the Lord be with you!"* (1 Samuel 17:37)

5) GO WITH WHAT WORKS

David won't go to war with untested means when he has tested means at his disposal... *"So Saul clothed David with his armor, and he put a bronze helmet on his head; he also clothed him with a coat of mail. David fastened his sword to his armor and tried to walk, for he had not tested them. And David said to Saul, 'I cannot walk with these, for I have not tested them.' So David took them off."* (1 Samuel 17:38-39)

When you're new in a field like sales for example, most companies will provide you with the approach they want you to take, the message they want you to deliver, the tactics to use, even the goals to set.

It's perfectly normal to emulate what they're doing before you deviate from their model. However, if you already know what brings good success, especially that which far exceeds expectations, then go with that.

What have you already proven out in your life? When I started selling copiers in British Columbia, I was given a bedroom community as my territory. The big boys got Vancouver. I was new and got a couple small towns an hour away. It's where I learned to sell. It's where I learned to trust God in my daily work. I learned how to thrive in a small community.

About eight years later, after being out of the industry for a couple years, I moved to the big city of Toronto and got a job selling copiers in the big city. So much opportunity, how could I not succeed?

Well, over the next eight months, that question was answered as I barely eked out a living. I was in a totally different environment than I was used to and even though I was selling the same brand of copiers as before, I was failing miserably. I returned to British Columbia with my tail between my legs.

Two years later, when I moved to the Nashville, TN area, I applied for a job selling copiers in downtown Nashville. Not because I ever wanted to sell copiers again, but because one day when driving through the downtown area on I-40, the Holy Spirit pointed out an office building / warehouse facility and said, *"That's where you're going to work!"*

I decided to see what kind of business was there, and when I found out it was selling copiers, I let Him know that I didn't really want to do that again. But I knew enough to obey, so I went to their office and asked if they were hiring.

As it turned out, they had been running an ad, but had just hired the former sales manager from Xerox to fill that position. It was then that the VP asked me if I would consider a rural territory, where they had not had much success.

I jumped at the chance. I knew that what they perceived as a slim opportunity, would be a gold mine for me because I already knew how to prosper in the smaller town environment and its rural surroundings.

I knew the victories I had won some 3,000 miles away in somewhat rural British Columbia and this seemingly lesser opportunity would be like one of those to me.

By end of my first year, I had set a record for most copiers sold in a single year and was promoted to sales manager!

6) PREPARE...

"Then he took his staff in his hand; and he chose for himself five smooth stones from the brook, and put them in a shepherd's bag, in a pouch which he had, and his sling was in his hand." (1 Samuel 17:40) David didn't run headlong into battle without preparation. The tools he readied for himself have implications for the world of business and especially for negotiating...

Four Powerful Tools for Success in Sales & Negotiating

I) Shepherd's staff: A staff was primarily used to bring the sheep in for closer inspection and to guide them. In business, asking questions becomes the tool of choice for closer inspection, learning more about your prospect's objectives and guiding them to the desired conclusion.

II) Stones: David knew that Goliath had four brothers and brought one stone for each of them. My five smooth stones will be the major points that focus on their vulnerabilities and reveal their pain. I will have one solid stone to go for the known weakness but be prepared for a few more that may be revealed during the negotiations.

For example, back in the days when Xerox had a virtual monopoly on the copier market, I competed against them almost every single time. I would go prepared with my best foot forward, but I always carried a few extra smooth stones in my briefcase.

On one such occasion, a prospect misrepresented the offer Xerox had made to him. I knew he was being dishonest because I knew the pricing and contract terms for every model Xerox offered, and I carried copies of each contract with me. They were in my "pouch of stones", just in case.

When he falsely claimed that Xerox was giving him a free, two-month trial and wanted to see if I would match that, I pulled out my copy of their contract and showed him that the sixty-day trial period they were offering was not free but did allow him to cancel at that time without penalty.

I politely gave him an offramp while completely slaying his claims. With nothing left to counter me with, he signed a contract and gave me a check.

III) Shepherd's bag: My bag is where I will conceal my "stones" until it is the opportune time to release them. It usually doesn't take everything you have, to win the sale or conclude a successful negotiation. But it's always good to keep something in reserve. You don't need to reveal everything you know, up front. But be prepared, just in case.

IV) Sling: My sling is my delivery method. Shrewd but kind. Swift but not hasty. Powerful but humble. Some folks need a lot of help on how they deliver their selling or negotiating points. Knowing when to release certain facts (timing) is also critical to your success.

St. Augustine of Hippo was a prominent church leader in the 4th and 5th centuries. One of the things he taught, was what he called, Grammar, Logic and Rhetoric.

As he explained it, "grammar" was the sum total of the knowledge you had on a given topic. "Logic" was the ability to connect those points of knowledge into a logical or cohesive argument. And finally, "rhetoric" was the art of delivering those points in an emotionally, compelling way.

Those three things correspond with what Solomon referred to over and over again as, Knowledge, Wisdom and Understanding.

A lot of folks are smart and have vast amounts of knowledge but struggle to make their point in a succinct and clear way. They don't have the logic part figured out, nor the understanding.

Others have great logic skills and are good at arguing with them, but don't have sufficient knowledge and are easily defeated with facts.

The one skill that is most persuasive is not knowledge, nor sound logic. It is what Augustine called "rhetoric" and Solomon called, "understanding".

May I suggest that you prepare your sling in such a way as to be obviously knowledgeable, soundly logical and emotionally compelling. Don't rely on just one of the three. It might work, but then again, it might not. It depends on what the other party has. Practice your sling skills of knowledge, wisdom and understanding until you can with confidence, slay your Goliath in the open field.

7) INITIATE THE CONTACT… *"And he drew near to the Philistine."* (1 Samuel 17:40) When you're prepared, initiate contact. He who frames the argument, usually wins. Progress on your terms, not the other person who usually is not thinking strategically. Start the process when you're ready, not on someone else's timetable.

One of the larger contracts I ever got was with a company whose president had informed me they had been stuck at $22 million in revenue for three years and he wanted help to get past that.

I flew out there to do a three-day analysis of his sales team and process. On day one, he introduced me to his Executive Vice President and politely stepped out of the conversation. That gentleman, I'll call Vick (not his real name), brought me into his office to get the ball rolling and begin making introductions.

When the door was closed, in a very accusing tone, Vick asked me what my angle was. He assumed I was scheming something and went straight for my jugular. When I reiterated why I was there, he asked me for my written agenda for the next three days.

He was attempting to establish control on his terms, but the terms he wanted were not the way I operated. I told him that I didn't use an agenda.

He demanded that I provide him with a written agenda for the next three days to which I responded again that I didn't use a written agenda.

That's when it got a bit testy. He said, "I've got a pen and a pad of paper. I want a written agenda!"

I replied as firmly, "I have a pen and a pad of paper, and I don't use a written agenda!"

Somehow my pushback earned some respect with him and by the end of three days, I was asked to submit a proposal for corporate training.

On my flight home, I told the Lord that I didn't want the headache. It simply wasn't the kind of client I wanted to work with. The Lord quietly whispered, *"He's your assignment"*, to which I immediately replied that if I had to work with them, there would be no discounts, despite the fact that it would be my biggest training contract ever!

When I came back with my proposal that ended up being over $200K, Vick demanded a guarantee. Because I had heard from God and knew that He had sent me there, I told Vick and the CEO, that if they wanted a guarantee, they should buy a toaster, as I had no control over the policies under which their team would operate.

I was awarded the contract and that year, we went to $30 million, breaking through the $22 million dollar barrier they hadn't been able to exceed for the previous three years.

8) LET THE OTHER PERSON PUT THEIR CARDS ON THE TABLE FIRST... *"So the Philistine came, and began drawing near to David, and the man who bore the shield went before him."* (1 Samuel 17:41) David initiated contact just enough to get Goliath to reveal his hand, so to speak.

David could see by Goliath's response that he was in fear because he felt he needed more than just himself to defeat this kid. Furthermore, the man who bore the shield could only defend Goliath's lower part, which revealed his vulnerability – his head. (Great strategy)

"And when the Philistine looked about and saw David, he disdained him; for he was only a youth, ruddy and good-looking. So the Philistine said to David, 'Am I a dog, that you come to me with sticks?'" (1 Samuel 17:42-43) Notice that Goliath saw the stick which may

have been meant to be a diversion of attention, because the stones were hidden in his pouch.

9) LOOK FOR WEAKNESSES…
*"And the Philistine cursed David **by his gods**."* (1 Samuel 17:43) Not all your negotiations will necessarily be with friendly prospects. In life, we sometimes find ourselves in need of shrewd skills, not to wrongfully take advantage of a less skilled person, but to rightfully protect and defend a just position.

In this case, Goliath just confirmed his major weakness which was his dependence on false gods that have no real power. Adding to his lack of moral or spiritual authority, was the fact that he displayed his natural weakness which was likely poor agility and needing another soldier to protect him with a shield. That exposed his greatest natural weakness, his oversized, easy to hit with a stone, head.

Talk is cheap
"And the Philistine said to David, "Come to me, and I will give your flesh to the birds of the air and the beasts of the field!" (1 Samuel 17:44) Goliath then tries to instill fear in David, which in reality was a further reflection of his own fear. David could see how afraid Goliath was by his armor, his armor bearer, his calling out to false gods and his attempt at bullying with words… a good indicator of a coward.

David Responds…
"Then David said to the Philistine, 'You come to me with a sword, with a spear, and with a javelin. But I come to you in the name of the Lord of hosts, the God of the armies of Israel, whom you have defied.'" (1 Samuel 17:45) David contrasts Goliath's physical weapons with the one true God who Goliath has defied. That instills further fear into Goliath because no doubt he was aware of

Israel's history and how they dealt with giants successfully in the past.

10) DECLARE THE OUTCOME...

"THIS DAY the Lord will deliver you into my hand, and I will strike you and take your head from you. And THIS DAY I will give the carcasses of the camp of the Philistines to the birds of the air and the wild beasts of the earth, that all the earth may know that there is a God in Israel. Then all this assembly shall know that the Lord does not save with sword and spear; for the battle is the Lord's, and He will give you into our hands." (1 Samuel 17:46-47) Notice the fact that David gave a definite time... NOW! If this was a game of poker, David just saw Goliath's bet and raised it significantly!

There is something very powerful about declaring the outcome before you engage the sale, the negotiation, or the battle. First of all, it galvanizes your commitment. Others hear it which further obligates you to succeed.

Secondly it inspires your allies and scares your enemies. In business, the other party is not your enemy, but starting the negotiation with a statement expressing confidence that there will be a mutually beneficial outcome reduces tension and creates a positive climate for negotiations.

11) RUN TOWARD THE CHALLENGE

"So it was, when the Philistine arose and came and drew near to meet David, that David hurried and **ran toward the army** *to meet the Philistine."* (1 Samuel 17:48) Never falter in the presence of your enemy. As the saying goes, "Never let them see you sweat." Once the decision is made... Launch!

Up until this point, it's all been talk. David was smaller and more agile than the behemoth Goliath and running at him most likely unnerved him. Goliath hadn't seen that kind of courage before. It reminds me of the little dog I saw chase a bear out of the back yard. The dog was no match for the bear, but the fact that the dog ran after him, made the bear retreat.

12) KNOCK OVER THE LEAD DOMINO

"Then David put his hand in his bag and took out a stone; and he slung it and struck the Philistine in his forehead, so that the stone sank into his forehead, and he fell on his face to the earth. So David prevailed over the Philistine with a sling and a stone, and struck the Philistine and killed him." (1 Samuel 17:49) In sales and negotiations it is critical to identify the greatest vulnerability, their most significant pain point, and direct your cold, hard facts (stone(s)) there.

"And when the Philistines saw that their champion was dead, they fled." (1 Samuel 17:51) It's the lead domino effect, because once you demolish the biggest vulnerability, the rest of the objections will fall much easier. When David exploited Goliath's weakness and killed him, it struck fear into the Philistine army who immediately fled. The big domino had fallen… The rest would easily fall.

In business, the biggest vulnerability a prospect feels is the missing piece that's holding them back from something they really want or need. That could be the right sales strategy to break through to the next level. It could be the right process that will eliminate high costs and give them profitability.

If they only knew what the missing link was and where to get it and knew it would work, they would already be doing it. But they don't. The missing link is the lead domino. Solve that and everything else is chit chat.

If you can help them believe that what you're offering is the missing link to what they're trying to achieve, and if you can show that it is only available through the specific means or vehicle that you're offering, then all objections become irrelevant, and they will do whatever is necessary to get your offer.

Just like Israel still had to deal with the Philistines who ran away in fear after Goliath was killed, you'll probably still have a few details to work out when you're lead domino falls, but the hardest part will be behind you.

Leave No Doubt…
"But there was no sword in the hand of David. Therefore David ran and stood over the Philistine, took his sword and drew it out of its sheath and killed him, And David took the head of the Philistine and brought it to Jerusalem," (1 Samuel 17:50, 51, 54) David made sure that this was a done deal. He carried Goliath's head back to town to show everyone the threat had been neutralized and would not be returning.

Don't leave loose ends dangling when it comes to closing a deal. I met Judy online via Facebook on Friday. She lived about 625 miles west of me. We talked through the night for the next few nights and finally met face to face the following Tuesday, whereupon I asked her to marry me.
She accepted.

I was already scheduled to do an event with Zig Ziglar in Dallas a few days later, and Judy needed to get back to Mississippi, so I said to her, "I don't want you returning home, an unmarked woman." We went shopping for a nice diamond ring which we were able to get before I flew to Dallas.

You see, I knew people would be in shock that this man she just met, (me) proposed marriage and she accepted. I didn't want any doubt to creep into her mind or give any reason for others to think I wasn't serious. A beautiful diamond ring was my way of solidifying my offer. I left no doubt in her mind or anyone else's that I was serious.

I returned from Dallas a few days later and on Friday, exactly two weeks after we first met online, we were married. For us, it has been amazing, and I still have to pinch myself to make sure I'm not dreaming.

CHAPTER 7

The Coming Wealth Transfer
(Not Quite What You Think)

*"The **wealth of the sinner** is stored up for the righteous."* (Prov 13:22)

*"For God gives wisdom and knowledge and joy to a man who is good in His sight; but to the sinner **He gives the work of gathering and collecting, that he may give to him who is good before God.**"*
(Ecclesiastes 2:26)

The verses cited above are often quoted to suggest they refer to what is sometimes called, "the end time wealth transfer". However, that is not how anyone reading those words when written would have understood them, neither do I believe they infer that even now.

There is a passage of Scripture in Isaiah 60 that refers to the future of Israel and arguably to the church as well, where it states emphatically… *"the wealth of the Gentiles shall come to you."* (Isaiah 60:5)

It follows a time when *"darkness shall cover the earth, and thick darkness the peoples;"* When that happens, Isaiah says, *"the Lord will arise upon you, and His glory will be seen upon you. And nations shall come to your light, and kings to the brightness of your rising."* (Isaiah 60:2-3)

The way I understand that Scripture is that any massive wealth transfer coming to God's people corporately, happens **_after_** a time of thick darkness when his glory is then seen upon us in such a way as to attract the nations and kings of the world.

We're not there yet.

So rather than wait for this amazing time to come, which may be further away than you expect, why not find out how to make that a present reality now?

God offered that privilege to His people a few thousand years ago. In Deuteronomy 8:18, He says, *"And you shall remember the Lord your God, for it is* **He who gives you power to get wealth***, that He may establish His covenant which He swore to your fathers, as it is this day."*

In Isaiah 48:17, God says, *"I am the Lord your God,* **who teaches you to profit***, who leads you in the way you should go."*

And as if that wasn't convincing enough, Wisdom being personified in Proverbs 8:20-21 says, *"I traverse the way of righteousness, in the midst of the paths of justice,* **that I may cause those who love me to inherit wealth***, that I may fill their treasuries."*

As it turns out, His promises have no expiry date on them. They're in the contract so to speak. Paul said it this way in 2 Corinthians 1:20 … *"For all the promises of God in Him are Yes, and in Him Amen, to the glory of God through us."* It's up to us to act on them.

But here's what you MUST UNDERSTAND… the wealth spoken of in the last three verses I quoted, is real, tangible wealth, but generally speaking, it's <u>not going to suddenly and unexpectedly appear on your front porch or in your bank account</u>.

You're going to have to create value for folks.
And the more value you can create in an inverse relationship to cost, the more successful you will be. (See chapters 83 and 84 for specific strategy and formulas for maximizing value to create maximum profit.)

You don't have to invent some new gadget or technology to be successful. You can succeed by doing something quite ordinary in an extraordinary way. Back in the 70's, coffee shops were just plain diners. No real ambience. For fifty cents you could have a booth, meet with a client, and drink all the coffee you wanted.

Then along came Starbucks. Not my favorite company, but they took one of the most boring and uninteresting, everyday beverages and built an experience around it.

The ambience was totally different, very welcoming, attractive and totally unique. The coffee was better and had names we had never heard of. The whole experience was a bit exotic for most of us.

Unbeknownst to them, they actually were using a strategy modeled in the rainforest. You see, in the tropical rainforests there are over 10,000 species of trees, all of them consisting of the same basic elements (wood, leaves and flower / fruit). Yet, each species is unique, and unmistakably so.

What makes them unique?

It's the design.
It's how they combine the exact same elements as the tree of a different species right beside them to produce a totally different visual experience.

And it's not by chance.

It's hard coded in the business plan, that we call the seed, but that is a topic we cover elsewhere in the book. They take the same nutrients, same light, same CO_2 and rainwater, and one tree produces Brazil nuts while another produces mangoes.

The design sets them apart and is what attracts a loyal following of customers (birds, bees, animals, etc.) who appreciate and can take advantage of the product (fruit, nuts, nectar, etc.) that the tree has to offer.

Starbucks broke the mold of the traditional coffee shop like you might have seen portrayed on the Seinfeld TV show. They created a totally different design that people were willing to pay for, and now have 2 ½ times as many locations as there are Burger King locations!

The big lesson here my friend is that you don't have to invent something the world has never seen before. You can take the mundane and redesign the experience, deliver it with excellence and do phenomenally well.

I tell you this for a reason… I want everyone to know that wealth and success is within reach of anyone. You already possess the God given raw materials to make a go of just about anything.

There are basics for success, and you have what it takes to learn those and provide very well for you and your family, while advancing God's kingdom through generosity.

In Deuteronomy God says, He has given us the power (strength, ability) to get (produce, acquire and bring about) wealth, so it's **already in us**. You already have the ability in raw form.

What you most likely lack is either the knowhow (practical steps to take), the development of your God-given abilities (skills), or the belief that you can really succeed at that level.

But God does not lie. Indeed, He cannot. (Hebrews 6:18) To address the "knowhow issue" he promised to teach us how to profit and those instructions are largely found in His book of instructions, we call the Bible.

I've been studying His Word as it relates to work and business for decades and it has been my primary "go to" source for increasing sales, building teams and starting and growing a business. If you'd like to tap into over 30 years of research and a community of like-minded believers, check out our online mentorship site at **MichaelPink.com/Secrets**. It could change your life!

So, while the wealth of the wicked is indeed laid up for the just, the just for the most part, are going to have to go into the marketplace where the wealth is, reflect the glory of God in their business through service and innovation and win the battle for the hearts and minds of those they wish to serve.

And while they do that, they know that their earthly wealth will be left behind at death, but their skills and acquired wisdom will be with them for eternity.

Game-changing strategy: Don't wait for the wicked to voluntarily turn over their wealth to you for no good reason. Learn how to create convincing value so that they feel stupid not giving you money. (More on that in another chapter)

CHAPTER 8

The Generosity Factor

*"He who has **a generous eye, will be blessed**."* (Proverbs 22:9)

*"**Give and it shall be given unto you**, good measure, pressed down, shaken together and running over."* (Luke 6:38)

I don't look at Luke 6:38 as some kind of formula for wealth. I see it as a simple description of reality, stated by the one (Jesus Christ) that all Christians say they are trusting for their eternal future.

Having said that, you have to admit, it's a great offer. So is, *"Come unto me all you that labor and are heavy laden and I will give you rest"* (Matthew 11:28) and many other statements Jesus made that I could quote.

Our problem so often, if we're honest about it, is that we don't really believe the words we are reading. That's not because the One who spoke them is dubious or questionable. It's because we obviously don't know the One who spoke them, very well.

My wife has told me some amazing stories from her life and because I know her character, I without hesitation believe every word. Trust comes from knowing. The more connected you are to Jesus, the more you know Him and the easier it is to believe every single word He spoke, even if you don't yet understand it.

I chose the Luke 6:38 verse even though I know many folks will instantly put me in some version of what they call the prosperity gospel as if I think that God is the great vending machine in Heaven, ready to dispense material goods if we just put enough money in the heavenly vending machine (offering plate).

He is not that. He is holy and righteous and altogether good. People say that Jesus talked more about money than any other subject. I beg to differ.

Just because He used money or pearls or gold, etc., in a parable doesn't mean that was what the parable was about. He did talk about the Pearl of great price, the lost coin and talents of silver or gold, etc., but they were analogies for a greater message.

Having given my disclaimer, I must also tell you without embarrassment or shame, what happened to me in 1979 as a 24-year-old sales manager. It may be hard to believe, but I will not pretend it did not happen.

I had just been promoted to sales manager after 4 years in sales and insisted on a straight commission pay plan, based on performance.

It was coming to the end of my first quarter in that position and it had not gone well. I was falling behind financially. So much so, that I was feeling very stressed having just moved into a beautiful new custom home in a prestigious neighborhood that came with much higher financial obligations.

One night near the end of my first quarter, a life insurance salesman came to my home and sold me a term life insurance policy with a $13 monthly premium. He was very impressed with my home, my new Lincoln, etc., and asked how it was possible for me, being so young, to have what I had.

What he didn't know, was the check I wrote for $13 would only be good because I had overdraft protection. I was broke!

After he left, I went to bed, but around 3 or 4 AM, I awoke. That's normal for me now but had never happened to me when I was in my twenties.

So, I thought the Lord must want to talk to me. I got up, went downstairs, grabbed my Bible, and asked Him to speak to me from His Word and tell me what He wanted me to know.

Very clearly, He spoke to me to turn to Luke 6:38. At the time, I didn't even know if Luke 6 had that many verses, let alone know what it said.

When I read, *"Give and it shall be given to you…"* I thought there must be some mistake. My problem wasn't that I had too much money. I didn't have enough to cover a $13 check without using overdraft protection.

But here's the kicker… I knew Jesus and I believed Him, so that morning I drove to work looking for someone to give money to. I wanted to put a sign in the company parking lot, "Need Cash? Pull in Here!"

As it turned out, I was with one of my salesmen, and in the course of the day's travels, he mentioned that he needed $200 in the worst way to pay for car insurance.

I was so relieved that I found someone with a need, that I pulled out my checkbook and wrote him a check on the spot with the condition that he could never pay me back because, as I explained, it would mess everything up.

He thought I was very strange indeed but took the check and went on his way. That evening, I stopped by the office to pick something up and found my boss working late. He stopped me and said that he had seen how hard I'd been working and decided to give me a bonus on my next check of no less than $2,000! That was a "WOW" moment for me.

The next day, to prove to a naysayer in my life, that this was no coincidence, I went looking for more people to help. That day, I wrote two more checks for $100 each, one of which was at a place I cold called!

The craziest thing happened…
My team rallied and delivered in the next 48 hours a record month earning me a much bigger bonus. Plus, a school district called in a purchase order for the largest order our company had ever received, and it was my account!

Bottom line is that I earned over $10K in just a few days, totally catching me up and getting me well ahead. (That was 1979.)

I've got a ton more stories from my own life like that. I could fill this book with them. I chose this one because in many ways it was a beginning for me, where the Lord Himself woke me up and took me to His very own words, to show me the way.

I thought that would be worth sharing. I would encourage you to take your own journey with the Lord. Get alone with Him. Ask Him to speak to you and show you His path forward for you.

I'll tell you this...
One thing I have observed from all the wealthy clients I personally have coached or provided training for… They were all generous givers. None of them took a formulaic approach to giving. They had just learned that there was a connection between generosity and their own provision and decided to make it a way of life.

I realize that many wealthy people are not generous givers, but God's way for prosperous living involves freely giving with an open hand. Jesus said, *"It is more blessed to give than to receive."* (Acts 20:35) I believe He is simply describing reality, telling us the way things are, so we can cooperate with the way He made things if we so choose.

I don't see it as He's keeping score any more than He punishes people who jump out of a plane without a parachute or rewards them by saving their life if they use a parachute. It's just the way things work.

Success is far easier when you learn how things work and flow with them. The Apostle Paul described the way things work this way… *"He who sows sparingly will also reap sparingly, and he who sows bountifully will also reap bountifully."* (2 Corinthians 9:6)

Find a good field to sow in. Ask God to show you where you can give and open up the flow in your life. Obviously, your local church where you attend is a great starting point but look to be a blessing to others as well.

Generosity is a great game-changer when done in faith believing that He who promised is faithful. Try it. You won't be disappointed. After a while it becomes second nature. So do the blessings.

CHAPTER 9

Discovering The Genius in You…

*"I will praise You, for I am fearfully and **wonderfully made**; Marvelous are Your works, and that my soul knows very well."*
(Psalm 139:14)

*"What is man that You are mindful of him? For You have made him a **little lower than Elohim**, And You have crowned him with glory and honor."* (Psalm 8:4-5)

God did not make mankind in a way, that would occasionally produce a genius like an Einstein or Bach or a Michael Jordan in sports or a Martin Luther King among orators.

He did not create a race of people, (the human race), that every once in a while, had some glitch that resulted in genius talent, genius artisan, genius oratory, genius dance, genius music, genius ability to distill truth from dew.

No. The human race is a race of genius, but with different expressions.

Consider the animal kingdom… You don't see some lions that are talented hunters, but most lions just work for that lion. They do have a leader, but they can all hunt. They can all be stealthy and talented in the thing God made them to do.

You never hear one lion talking to another and saying, "Did you see the way Leo took down that gazelle?!?!?! That guy is crazy talented! Wish I could hunt like him!"

You never hear one eagle saying to another… "Look at Eddie… Always showing off. Riding those wind currents with such ease. Barely has to flap his wings. He just soars on high, like it was nothing. Not me man. I walk everywhere. Takes me longer, but it's safe AND I'm not talented like Eddie!"

NO. You will never hear that.

They see Eddie the Eagle soaring and they think, "I can do that!" because eagles were created to soar, not walk.

But the human race, (people), were made in the very image AND likeness of God. (Genesis 1:26) We can hunt AND soar. We can sing AND dance. We can do just about anything we put our mind to.

God made a race of geniuses, a little lower than God, or as the Youngs Literal translation of the Bible puts it, we *"lack a little of Godhead."* God put within each one of us, special gifts and abilities that we are to develop.

Sadly, we lost our genius over time, but it didn't cease to exist.

It got buried… Under lies. Lies told to us by our parents, by societal norms, by the ruling class, by our next-door neighbor. Most of the time, they were simply passing along a lie, that they believed to be true. And because of their sincerity, their own believable delusion, we bought into it as well.

But we can get out. Our genius can be… Reborn. Renewed. Restarted. Released. Again. But better, stronger, more powerful than ever.

Consider This… *"Christ in you, the hope of glory."* (Colossians 1:27) What does that mean?

He lives in us by invitation and His very presence within, gives us the HOPE of glory. What is glory? It's the magnificence of God. It's the genius or brilliance He encoded into all of us to discover.

And that dwells in you but is concealed. Concealed by doubt. Concealed by fear. Concealed by ignorance.

Too often we're afraid to manifest or demonstrate the magnificence of God, but that is our calling, our destiny, our great and longing joy.

That is why it is a hope and not a guaranteed fact. Because manifesting the magnificence of God, (the love of God, the wisdom of God, the very power of God, etc.), scares us. Can we really do that? Are we being too presumptuous?

We have so lost the knowledge that we were created in the image AND likeness of God. And it is the very presence of Christ within us that teaches us and restores us to the right knowledge of God.

And as that happens, we change. We become new. Something we weren't before. Something wonderful (to the extent we allow that to happen) and beautiful and glorious.

And as that seed of knowledge grows into a tree, we begin to manifest His glory and His magnificence which He has given to all who wish to have it, and have the courage to take hold of, and grow into it.

We are being presumptuous NOT to manifest His glory. We presume that His magnificence (glory) is not worthy of emulation, that our own is sufficient. In doing so, we miss the mark.

Recognizing, accepting, and tapping into the hard-wired genius within you is a game-changer. Don't delay. Step into it now – without hesitation!

I have SO MUCH more to share with you. Keep reading.

CHAPTER 10

How Freshly Poured Hot Wax Can Save Your Business

*"I want you to **be wise in what is good**, and **simple concerning evil**. And the God of peace will soon crush Satan under your feet."*
(Romans 16:19-20)

Guy Kawasaki said something like "every business-oriented person needs to pour hot wax in their ears so they will stop hearing the continuous stream of bad news". I think he's right. We not only need to remove the clutter of bad news, but we also need to fill our mind with good information.

Deep in the Amazon during the hot, dry season, scientists were surprised to discover that the dry season is actually the "good season" for tree and plant growth.

That's right, the Amazon goes through an annual period of "recession" (shortage of water) lasting several months and yet those same regions actually "green up" during that time. This was not true of cleared areas where cattle grazed and grass grew, but in the rainforest, the dry season is a time of rapid growth.

Here's how it works… The forest soil retains much of the moisture from the rainy season down as far as 30 feet where the roots can still access all the water they need.

When the sun is shining, it provides the power to fuel the production process of wood, leaves, fruit, nuts, etc. In Scripture, water is analogous to information. *"For the earth shall be full of the **knowledge of the Lord as the waters** cover the sea."* (Isaiah 11:9) *"That He might sanctify and cleanse her with the* *washing of water by the word."* (Ephesians 5:26) and light is analogous to faith and revelational wisdom which power innovation and growth.

What you have with that example from the Amazon, is a picture of a person or a company who stores up information or resources (*"Wise people store up knowledge."* Proverbs 10:14) to be used when everyone else is in recession or retreat.

J.D. Rockefeller and Andrew Carnegie made their moves during the great depression of the 1870's. Conrad Hilton and J. Paul Getty made their moves during the Great Depression of the 1930's. They advanced when everyone else was retreating.

For the record, I am not holding these men up as examples we should follow, but the Bible does say in Luke 16:8, *"For the sons of this world are more shrewd in their generation than the sons of light."*

Which way are you headed? Care to advance with me? If you will shut off the spigot of bad news and fill your mind with good information you can enter the best time of growth you've ever experienced despite what everyone else is experiencing.

When most people are retreating, it's the best time to be advancing. That fact is a game-changing strategy. Think about it. One of the first expenses people cut in tough times, is advertising. If you keep advertising and putting your best foot forward during slow times, you will pick up a ton of customers that would normally have gone to your competition.

The short and long-term impacts of advertising when others are retreating due to recession, fear, etc., have been the subject of numerous studies.

McGraw Hill studied the recession that occurred between 1980 and 1985. Their study involved 600 companies from 16 different industries. Some maintained their ad spend. Some chose to actually increase it. Others either reduced or cut their ad budget altogether.

The findings were astonishing. They confirmed that companies who maintained or increased their advertising during the adverse economic times in the early '80's, experienced 256% higher sales than their competitive counterparts after the recession.

On the flip side, companies who retreated and chose not to advertise during the economic downturn, experienced virtually 0% increase in market share and a modest rise in sales of just 18% on average once the economy regained traction.

By comparison, those companies who chose to be bold and advance while others were retreating, experienced a sales increase rate that was 14 times higher than those who held back. This strategy really is a game-changer!

The resulting expression arising out of that stark revelation became a mantra in the advertising world… "In times of prosperity, you should advertise. In times of hardship, you **must** advertise."

In tough times, there is less competition for market space. I am not sure how long our current craziness will last, but I do know that it is the best window of opportunity I've ever lived in!

If you have ever wanted to know how to prosper during turbulent times and if you've ever been interested in being used by God to help others survive and prosper when the world is in decline, we do have a private mentorship site with volumes of online training and LIVE events.

Come by and check it out at MichaelPink.com/Secrets. We've made it so affordable, that anyone who wants to, can join, learn, and network. Hope to meet you in there.

CHAPTER 11

The Power of NOW

*"**In the valley of indecision**, lay the skeletal remains of many a worthy plan"* (Michael Q. Pink)

*"**Now** faith is the substance…"* (Hebrews 11:1)

*"Behold, **now** is the accepted time; Behold, **now** is the day of salvation."* (2 Corinthians 6:2)

*"And do this, knowing the time, that **now it is high time** to awake out of sleep; for **now** our salvation is nearer than when we first believed."* (Romans 13:11)

Would you like a real big secret for success?

It has to do with the concept of "NOW". It's easy to believe for something far off, or that is not directly in front of us. We struggle with the NOW. We can believe for a bright future, someone to get saved, etc., but when we step into the NOW, well that's a different story. Why?

We don't operate in the now…
Jesus told His disciples NOT to say that the harvest was four months off. He said it was NOW. It's ALWAYS NOW. But we are like the horse pulling the cart with the carrot dangling in front of him. We chase the future. We believe in the future, but God wants us to take the future into the present moment (the NOW).

Faith operates in the NOW. Hope believes in the future, but FAITH believes the future promise or hope, is NOW. Not tomorrow. Not in some imaginary scenario. It only operates in the NOW. NOW is the day of Salvation. NOW is the day of deliverance. NOW is the day of revival.

NOW is also the time for witty inventions! NOW is the time to succeed in your business or perhaps to launch it. NOW is the time for taking territory. Operate with a NOW mindset and take action NOW.

Hesitation Valley is a place where hope springs eternal, but faith is nowhere to be seen. They've circled the wagons, built their bonfire, and sang songs about their faith and the bright future they're hoping for.

That's Hesitation Valley. It looks good and sounds good, but will be the end of you, just like it was for Abraham's father, Terah when he remained in Haran. Where he died. The time to leave Hesitation Valley is NOW.

Victory is determined in the NOW moment...
It may be manifest in a future moment, but it must take place in the NOW. You will know when you believe that the victory you've been hoping for has moved into the NOW because you will take action.

Hope plans for the future and gets excited about it. Hope even tells people about the future, but faith, brings it into the now. That's why faith has "works", and faith without works is dead. (James 2:17)

Faith REQUIRES action and without action, you're not operating in faith. At best, it is hope. Action by definition and by observation of the obvious, can only be accomplished in the NOW moment. Actions are always accomplished in the NOW.

Doesn't the Bible say in Hebrews 11… NOW, faith is… the SUBSTANCE of things HOPED for… the EVIDENCE of things not seen? Faith ALWAYS has substance.

Noah had faith and the substance was the ark he built. Abraham had faith and the substance that was seen, was him tying Isaac to the woodpile for sacrifice.

Every example of faith in the Bible had an observable action with it. By faith, Isaac blessed Jacob and Esau concerning things to come. Isaac's faith was demonstrated with an action in the present moment, though the fruit of his faith was manifested in later years. Same was true of Joseph who gave instructions (an action) concerning his bones after he died.

We must move from HOPE to FAITH.
We must quit being satisfied with the carrot in front of us and start seizing the NOW moment. NOW IS THE DAY OF OPPORTUNITY. NOW is the day to act on what we say we believe. Tomorrow is hope, and that's good and necessary, but TODAY we live by FAITH in the NOW.

Every successful entrepreneur I know of, transitioned from hoping they would one day succeed, to having the faith to act. And that involved risk.

Risk is a very real component of faith because we can experience setbacks and failures while walking in faith. You will never experience the success or victory you dream of, by mere talk or even just by declaration. You must take action.

What does that look like?
When I was in my twenties and dead broke after losing my daughter to death, losing my first real business, my marriage, my homes and car, etc., and was staying at a friend's home for survival, I was desperate to see God rescue me.

One evening, I went to a home meeting where another young man was asking for prayer for his knee. After folks prayed for him, they broke for coffee and cookies.

I was pretty cynical at that time and thought to myself, if he really had faith to be healed, he would jump up NOW and do what he couldn't previously do.

At that moment, the Holy Spirit challenged me to do the same kind of thing regarding my finances. I was two months behind on a bank loan payment and they wanted paid and kept calling me.

I felt like the Holy Spirit challenged me to do what I was critical of the young man for not doing. I was to take the action corresponding to my "belief" that God would help me financially.

So, I determined that first thing the next morning, I would drive to the bank, ask for the loan officer handling my account, tell him I had the money for payments (roughly $1,500), and then open my wallet and start counting out the cash.

What made this idea particularly challenging was that I had NO CASH in my wallet, or anywhere else for that matter. But I determined to do exactly that, knowing that I would appear to be either a fool or a deceiver if I told the loan officer I had the money in my wallet, opened it up to pay him, and there was nothing there.

The next morning without telling anyone my predicament or intentions, I headed off to do just that. No one knew I was two months behind on my bank payment because it's just not the kind of thing you tell folks.

On my way to the bank, I stopped by the place where I had been staying, to get something. While there, I ran into a good friend who said that he had just been seeking the Lord that morning and was supposed to give me a check. It was for $2,000. I carried on to the bank, cashed the check and made my $1,500 payment.

Say what you want, but I remain convinced that God responded to my faith in a very unexpected way and that need was met. The point here is the same hope for the future must transition to faith in the NOW and that is always and only demonstrated by corresponding action.

I'm just as challenged by this word as you may be, so let's be wise, take action, and make the most of every opportunity, because the days are evil, (Ephesians 5:16) and now is the day of salvation.

Bringing your faith into the NOW and taking action, is a game-changing strategy that will give you a huge advantage over those who delay.

CHAPTER 12

Godly Indignation (Rocket Fuel for Your Business)

"What diligence it produced in you, what clearing of yourselves, **what indignation***, what fear, what vehement desire, what zeal, what vindication!"* (2 Corinthians 7:11)

"By your sword you shall live and serve your brother. But [the time shall come] when you will grow restive and break loose, and **you shall tear his yoke from off your neck***."* (Genesis 27:40 AMPC)

"Shake yourself from the dust, arise; Sit down, O Jerusalem!
Loose yourself from the bonds of your neck*,*
O captive daughter of Zion!" (Isaiah 52:2)

Have you had enough yet? Things aren't going to change for the better until and unless you decide you've had enough of the status quo.

I'm speaking of the kind of indignation that Isaac said his son Esau would eventually get when he became restless and dissatisfied with life as it was. It's the kind of disgust that as Isaac told Esau, would make him **tear the yoke off** his neck! Does that sound passive to you?

Sometimes, you just need to say, "Enough is enough!" It's appropriate at times to get angry at something. There was a guy at church who got mad at the local church leadership for turning what was intended to be a house of prayer into a club atmosphere with an emphasis on retail.

So, one day he'd had enough of all their buying and selling, and he knocked over their displays, spilled their coffee drinks and made a whip out of an electric cord and drove the vendors out of the building.

OK, so maybe that didn't happen at a church, but it's very close to what Jesus did when he made a whip and drove the merchants out of the temple, because they had turned what was supposed to be a house of prayer into a den of thieves. He was indignant.

I doubt that He had never seen it before, but the day came when it was too much, when it was time to make a statement that would be remembered for time immemorial.

A righteous indignation is like rocket fuel. When lit, it will take you further in a short time than any conventional means you may know of. So, when are you going to quit tolerating the unacceptable?

When are you going to draw your own line in the sand, and determine from this day forward things will be different... that you will no longer tolerate lack? When will you decide that you'll no longer tolerate poor performance, lack of sales, sloppy workmanship, poor customer service, high staff turnover, etc.?

When a condition or circumstance has persisted for some time, robbing you of opportunity, promotion, sales, etc., and the things you have brought to bear against them have not worked, maybe it's time to become indignant.

I am not suggesting you turn that indignation against a person, but rather against the result you are currently experiencing or the spirit, attitude or mindset that is locking you into that negative and limiting condition.

Get mad at poor performance. Be hostile towards the spiritual forces arrayed against you. They would kill you if they could. Don't be nice to them. Paul told us to take up a sword against them. That sword of course is the Word of God, but he chose a violent metaphor.

He could have compared the Word of God to a flower if he wanted, but Paul was letting the Ephesians know they were in a serious fight with spiritual wickedness at multiple levels. It was time to bring out the sword imagery and wield it!

About 40 years ago, over a very short period of time, I had buried my first born, lost my marriage, lost my business, my home, my car, even my furniture. I was dead broke, over nearly a quarter million dollars in debt and that's just the losses I'm willing to talk about in print.

I moved to Toronto, got a job in sales and that winter, the company took us to a ski resort for a weekend of training and recreation. I had never skied before but thought I would give it a try.

I climbed up the mountain, strapped on cross country skis (which are not meant for downhill skiing) and began my rapid descent down the mountain side. Being a complete novice, and not having the right kind of skis, I ended up falling many times and actually doing better going backwards (quite by accident) than when facing forward.

That night I went for a walk on the lake which was dotted with ice fishing holes and the lake ice was beginning to melt. I began contemplating the idea of the ice giving way to my weight, and the lake swallowing me up. I was depressed, defeated, and deflated. I wanted out of emotional pain.

As I looked heavenward to the starry sky on that crisp night in early March, it was like I could see a horde of demonic powers above me, desiring very much to push me through the ice, but of course, unable to.

What I saw that night, aroused indignation in me. Something wanted me dead, and I was not going to comply. I got angry and yes, I yelled back at them. I reminded them of how David defeated Goliath and somehow, with God's great help, I would find a way to defeat the enemies of my soul and the circumstances that were slowly drowning me.

The next morning walking to the hotel meeting room for our final day of training, I saw that mountain looming in front of me, the snow on its crest, gleaming in the morning sun. It felt like it was taunting me, telling me it was still there, and I was still defeated.

What I'm about to tell you might seem strange to you, but some of you will get it. I stared straight at that mountain and told it, I was coming back that night and I would ski down it until I could ski down it blindfolded! I was indignant. I was angry. And I was determined to change the narrative!

By the time classes were over and the final evening meal, we were all enjoying some down time in the lodge, when I suddenly remembered what I had said to the mountain. I asked my sales manager if he would go skiing with me one last time and he obliged, despite the fact that it was almost midnight, and I still couldn't ski without falling down.

We climbed to the top of the mountain and strapped on our skis and proceeded downhill. I made it without falling! Not easy to do with cross-country skis. But we weren't finished.

We went back to the top, strapped on our skis again, but this time I asked to borrow his thick, black, scarf. I tied it around my head, wearing it like a blindfold and couldn't see a thing. Then I asked him to give me a push to get me started. There's nothing quite like it. Skiing down a mountain, blindfolded at midnight wearing the wrong skis and I was a novice.

The rush of the wind as I raced down the hill. The utter silence of the moment other than the whisking of my skis as I glided downward. The questions that race through your mind, such as, "Am I headed towards any trees? How much further to the bottom?" come to mind.

Not only did I make it to the bottom without falling, but when I got there, I tore off the scarf and looked back at the mountain. It was like it was screaming "That was luck!"

Well, you can probably guess what I did… I hiked back up one more time, strapped the skis and the blindfold back on and raced to the bottom unaided by the benefit of sight or skill.

When I arrived at the bottom of the hill the second time, unharmed and unfallen, although fairly close to a tree, I turned back to the mountain and spoke to it. I told it I defeated it and I would also with God's great help defeat all the other seemingly insurmountable challenges in my life at that time.

It was indignation that ignited the passion in me to face my fears, take the risks and ultimately defeat those enemies. In the next chapter, I'm going to blow your mind with the strategy Esau used to break the yoke off of his neck.

CHAPTER 13

Destroying The Yoke with Prosperity

*"It shall come to pass in that day that his burden will be taken away from your shoulder, and his yoke from your neck, And the **yoke will be destroyed** because of the anointing oil."* (Isaiah 10:27 NKJV)

There was a time in Israel's history that the Assyrians oppressed them terribly, but God promised in Isaiah 10 that the burden of that oppression would be lifted, and the yoke of bondage would be destroyed.

Some have argued that it is the "anointing oil" that breaks the yoke of any kind of bondage. I understand them to mean, that when God's Spirit comes upon you in a special way, you will be able to destroy the yokes of bondage holding you back.

But exactly, what anointing oil is Isaiah speaking of?

It's interesting to note that the Young's Literal translation says it this way… *"And destroyed hath been the yoke, **because of prosperity.**"* I want to open your eyes to something you may never have seen… Have you ever noticed how you carry yourself when you are really prospering? There's a certain confidence in your stride, a stability in your step.

There's something about success that sets in motion major life changes and throws off a multitude of yokes.

Consider the person who starts a business, working part-time from home while staying at a job they hate. They keep the job they are very dissatisfied with because they need the income, but they are miserable.

Then it happens… Their part-time income exceeds their full-time income from their job. They no longer need to be under the yoke of the employer who demands long hours and other sacrifices for little extra consideration.

The "anointing oil" as the New King James Version calls it, or the "prosperity" as the Youngs Literal Translation calls it, are really one and the same thing.

The Hebrew word translated "anointing" in Isaiah 10:27 is "shemen" which is almost always translated as "oil", as in olive oil, which was used to anoint kings and priests for service.

Now, let's use a little sanctified common sense… Will physical olive oil destroy a wooden yoke? Of course not. In fact, oil preserves wood.

The words "yoke" and "oil" (shemen) are used metaphorically. It would be more accurate to translate verse 27 this way…
"And at that day shall his burden be taken away from off thy shoulder, and his yoke from off thy neck: and the yoke shall be destroyed **because of the oil**.*"*

That still doesn't make sense unless you understand that… <u>**oil was considered liquid gold**</u> and was the backbone of the import-export trade in the ancient world.

It was used as prize money in the ancient Olympics. In fact, the best runner got 2500 kilos of high-quality oil which was almost 5 years wages and the winner of the chariot race got 5000 Kilos which was close to 10 years wages!

When you had beautiful, golden olive oil in abundance, you were wealthy, and you could shake off the yoke of bondage you'd been under to others, that were your source of provision, in exchange for servitude.

Consider a certain woman of the wives of the sons of the prophets in 2 Kings 4, who cried out to Elisha, saying, *"Your servant my husband is dead…, and the creditor is coming to take my two sons to be his slaves."*

Elisha said to her, *"What shall I do for you? Tell me, what do you have in the house?"* And she said, *"Your maidservant has nothing in the house but a jar of oil."*

Notice what Elisha told her… *"Go, borrow vessels from everywhere, from all your neighbors—empty vessels; do not gather just a few. And when you have come in, you shall shut the door behind you and your sons; then pour it into all those vessels and set aside the full ones."*

Elisha was preparing her for a miracle of provision. Instead of multiplying bread like Jesus did, Elisha was going to multiply the oil. This was amazing, not only for the miracle of it, but for what it represented. Elisha was going to multiply olive oil which was liquid gold and could easily be converted to physical silver or gold.

In fact, when she got all the empty vessels she could get from friends and neighbors, and they were all filled with this precious oil, he told her, *"Go,* **sell the oil and pay your debt;** *and you and your sons live on the rest."*

It was the oil that put her in a position of prosperity and broke the yoke of debt and bondage off her. And it is prosperity that will break off the yokes of bondage and debts facing you. It's like Solomon said in Ecclesiastes 10:19… *"Money answers everything!"*

When you demystify the anointing spoken of by Isaiah and understand that he was speaking of a common instrument of wealth called "oil", it puts the freedom and liberty from bondage that you seek, within your reach.

You're no longer depending on a mystical experience, valid as those can be, but rather, you can become indignant with your circumstances and with God's great wisdom and favor, walk out a path to prosperity that will provide you the freedom and provision needed to no longer be in bondage to anyone, anywhere.

CHAPTER 14

The Necessity of Desire

"Delight yourself also in the Lord, and He shall **give you the desires of your heart.***"* (Psalm 37:4)

"Therefore, I say unto you, **Whatever you desire**, *when you pray, believe that you receive them, and you shall have them."* (Mark 11:24)

"The **desire of the righteous** *will be granted."* (Proverbs 10:24)

*"***He will fulfill the desire** *of those who fear Him;"* (Psalm 145:19)

The Bible has much to say about desire. There are good desires and evil desires, but all desires have pull. They draw you to the object of your desire and they can sometimes draw the object of the desire to you. It's incumbent upon you to choose the right desires. I will proceed with that assumption.

When you delight yourself in the Lord by spending time consciously connecting with Him through His Word, or in worship, or in prayer or casual conversation with Him, I believe your heart will only desire what is good. Solomon said in Proverbs 11:23, *"The desire of the righteous is only good."* And it is those desires that the Lord is pleased to give you (Psalm 37:4)

The problem is that a lot of people lead muddled lives. Ask them what they want out of life, and they don't really know, or it's something vague, like happiness. It is very important to know what you want and to be able to express it simply and clearly.

In Mark 10:51, Jesus asked a blind man, *"What do you want me to do for you?"* It would seem the answer was obvious, but Jesus required the man to state what he wanted. He replied, *"Lord, that I might receive my sight."*

Jesus didn't heal him indiscriminately. The man needed to get clear on his desire, then crystalize it with words, at which point Jesus simply said, *"Your faith has made you whole."* If the man couldn't clarify what he desired, he couldn't have developed the faith to obtain it. You can't believe for something that you can't define.

Jesus said in Mark 11:24, *"Therefore, whatsoever things you DESIRE when you pray, believe that you receive them, and you will have them."* If you don't really know exactly what you desire, you really can't pray effectively for them. Learn to get clear on your desires before you throw up generic "feel good" prayers that accomplish nothing.

The same is true in business… Get crystal clear on what you desire, and the path becomes very clear. Doesn't mean you won't have obstacles or that it will be an easy ride, but it does mean that when you face opposition and temporary setbacks, you still have the desire pulling you forward.

Desire is the quality of wanting something bad enough, that you'll take action to bring it about. David wrote in Psalms 27:4 **"ONE THING I have desired of the Lord, THAT will I seek**: *That I may dwell in the house of the Lord All the days of my life, to behold the beauty of the Lord, And to inquire in His temple."* David was very clear about what he wanted most, and he became forever known as a man after God's own heart.

When David was young, his father Jesse sent him with some food to the army camp where his brothers were stationed opposite the Philistines and Goliath. It was there that David was told that whoever killed Goliath would receive great riches from the king, as well as his daughter and he would be exempt from taxes the rest of his life.

David could scarcely believe his ears. He asked two other soldiers to tell him what would be done for the man who killed Goliath. They both repeated the same things. David got really clear on the reward, confirmed that it was real and then set his heart on killing Goliath and collecting the reward. Later in life David wrote, *"my eye has seen its **desire** upon my enemies."* (Psalm 54:7) Surely this included Goliath.

David had the story told to him a total of three times, thus painting a picture of the desire clearly in his heart. The desire needed to be strong because it had to be equal to the task at hand. And it was more than equal.

The bigger the object of your desire, the stronger the desire must be. Think of it like muscular strength. The stronger you are, the more you can pull towards you. What do you desire to accomplish with your life? If you can't articulate that, you need only a tepid amount of desire to get you through the day.

You only have one life to live. Might as well make it count.

What do you desire to accomplish in this one life you have to live? Talk to the Lord about it. Marinate it in His Word. If it doesn't go against His Word and you sense His pleasure in it, then begin to strengthen that desire by thinking about it, researching, talking to others, get movies or songs or pictures that remind you and propel you towards that desire.

Shun those things that dampen your desire. Talk about it often, if only to yourself. Write out plans for making it happen and what will happen when that desire is met. Develop that desire in you so strongly that anyone who meets you, will know what you desire.

These days almost anyone can make a video about something using images and royalty free music. The more you're invested in it, the more you're going to stick with it when times are hard. Proverbs 13:12 says, *"Hope deferred makes the heart sick, but when the desire comes, it is a tree of life."*

As the hope of your desire tarries, refresh your soul with the knowledge that when it comes it will be like a tree of life to you, or as Proverbs 13:19 says, *"A desire accomplished is sweet to the soul."* So, get clear on your desire. Strengthen your desire. Never give up on your desire. And remember, it was Jesus Himself who said, *"If you abide in Me, and My words abide in you, you will **ask what you desire**, and **it shall be done** for you."* (John 15:7)

Never underestimate the power of desire!

CHAPTER 15

Hesitation – The Silent Dream Killer

*"**Do not hesitate** to go and enter to possess the land."* (Judges 18:9)

*"Elijah approached all the people and said, '**How long will you hesitate** between two opinions? If the Lord is God, follow Him; but if Baal, follow him.'"* (1 Kings 18:21)

*"Choose for yourselves **this day** whom you will serve… As for me and my house, we will serve the Lord."* (Joshua 24:15)

In my early twenties I took the admonition in James 1:5 to heart, that if any man lacked wisdom, let him ask of God and it would be given him. I read Proverbs and was inspired by Solomon and his wisdom, so I asked God if He would start giving me some proverbs like he did for Solomon.

The very first one He gave me was this… *"In the valley of indecision, lay the skeletal remains of many a worthy plan."* I have recalled it many times over the years when I seemed stuck in a place of indecision, and it helped me to make a decision and move forward. As I heard one man say, "God can't steer a parked car".

My good friend and mentor, Peter J. Daniels says, "We have been able to prove scientifically that **successful people make decisions quickly and change their mind rarely**, while unsuccessful people make decisions slowly and change their mind often."

Solomon once noted that *"He who observes the wind will not sow, and he who regards the clouds will not reap."* (Ecclesiastes 11:4) The cost of hesitation is a missed harvest. Remember this… **"The opportunity of a lifetime, only lasts for the lifetime of the opportunity."**

When the children of Israel hesitated to go into Canaan out of fear, God vowed that other than Joshua and Caleb, none of the adults over 20 years of age would ever enter it.

But apparently, they had heard the slogan, "God is a God of second chances", (a verse that appears nowhere in the Bible) and took it to mean that they could change their mind and go into the Promised Land anyway. They were after all… sorry.

However, when they tried to go in the next day, the Amalekites and Canaanites attacked and drove them back. Their opportunity had passed. Their hesitation killed the dream for them. The opportunity passed to the next generation. Don't make the same mistake.

In reality, second chances don't exist. Never have. Never will. Try going back to the town you grew up in, or the one you moved away from five years ago. You'll realize the truth of the expression, "You can never go home again", because nothing is static, and everything is always changing.

Don't despair. There will always be another first chance. It will be different from the one you missed. It might be better, and it might not. You don't know. So, when God brings an opportunity your way with a promise, don't hesitate. Take it.

There's a big difference between being hasty and being decisive. Indecision is often due to uncertainty. Certainty comes from knowing. When you know the facts, it's easy to decide. When you know what the outcome will be, it's even easier to decide.

But you don't always have all the facts or know for certain the outcome. Well guess what? Neither did Abram, when God told him to go to a land that he would show him.

It was more like… "I'll let you know when you get there. Just get started north." How could Abram have done that? He didn't have all the answers, but he knew God was leading him. He had total faith in God. THAT is what fills in the missing pieces… HAVING FAITH IN GOD!

I'm not talking about a saving faith that one day you'll go to Heaven. I'm talking about faith that knows that God is with you and will keep and guide you. When you have that super confident faith in God, it's easy to be decisive, even when you don't have the "how" questions answered.

When I first wrote the Bible Incorporated and called the printer to place my first order for 25,000 leather-bound, gold-leaf edged, brass-cornered, individually gift-wrapped books, I didn't have the money to photocopy even one book, let alone purchase 25,000!

The printer was astonished at the size of my order because, as he explained, most books in America never sell more than 5000 copies, and I was not a publisher. I was just a guy with a big basement and no distribution outlet. I was completely unknown in the publishing and retail book space.

The initial order was going to cost me around $100,000 and it would be due in 30 days from delivery. He urged me to reconsider the size of my order. I did. For about 10 seconds. Maybe less.

I put my hand over the phone and quickly asked the Lord about it. Apparently, God knew that I was not an established publishing company with a database and that most books from established publishers never sell more than 5000 copies over the life of the book. He even knew that I didn't have enough money to pay for 10% of the final price tag.

But He was good with it and gave me the go ahead. I didn't hesitate because although I had no idea how it was going to work out, I knew He did. My work, indeed, the work of God for anyone, is to **BELIEVE in Him** whom He (God the Father) sent. (John 6:29)

So, I proceeded with the order. God gave me a strategy and favor for pre-sales resulting in 7,000 books pre-sold and then He got me on national television, driving demand and I was able to pay for them in a satisfactory manner. We were sold out in eight months and ordered another 25,000 copies. This process was repeated over and over again.

Hesitation kills dreams. So, as John Maxwell says, "Find the source of your hesitation, and address it. You won't be able to move forward on the outside until you can move forward on the inside.

CHAPTER 16

The Power of "Understanding" How to Get It & Why It Matters!

*"Do not be like the horse or like the mule, **which have no understanding**, which must be harnessed with bit and bridle, Else they will not come near you."* (Psalm 32:9)

In the Parable of the Sower, Jesus said that some seed fell by the wayside; and the birds came and devoured them. He went on to explain, that anyone who hears the word of the kingdom, and DOES NOT UNDERSTAND it, will have that knowledge snatched away from them.

However, those WITH UNDERSTANDING will reap a 30, 60, even 100-fold increase.

It's incumbent upon us who preach and teach, or sell and market our goods, to be conscientious to cause understanding. You will know when you've gained or caused understanding by whether or not action is taken. For example, in Proverbs 24:30-34 we read,

> *"I went by the field of the lazy man, And by the vineyard of the man **devoid of understanding**; And there it was, all overgrown with thorns; Its surface was covered with nettles; Its stone wall was broken down. When I saw it, I considered it well; I looked on it and received instruction: A little sleep, a little slumber, A little **folding of the hands to rest**; So shall your poverty come like a prowler, And your need like an armed man."*

The distinguishing mark of the man <u>devoid of understanding</u>, was his lack of action. It's not that he didn't intellectually grasp the concept that things left to themselves, deteriorate. He just didn't care. Caring is an emotional response that resides in the heart.

God told Job, *"Who has put wisdom in the mind, or who has given* **understanding to the heart?***"* (Job 38:36) Proverbs tells us to **"Apply our heart to understanding"** and to fools it says, *"Be of* ***an understanding heart"***

In business, understanding answers the question, "What does this mean to me?" Have you ever made a presentation or delivered a quote for work, or for the purchase of your product or service, and then not heard back from them? Your offer made perfect sense. The numbers added up. You know you had the better offer. But they didn't buy and won't return your call.

The most common reason folks don't take action that is demonstrably in their best interest, is because their heart has not been activated. They do not understand. Yes, they can follow your reasoning, but they don't see themselves inside your picture. It's got to matter to them before they will take action.

Without understanding of the heart, you're flying blind. Paul prayed for the church in Ephesus that the **"eyes of their understanding** *would be enlightened, that they would know…"* (Ephesians 1:18)

Knowing comes from seeing. That's true in the physical realm but it's also true in the conceptual realm. It's your job to bring light to the eyes of your prospect's heart.

Logic, though very important, for most people is secondary. 90% of the decision is made in the heart and if you don't win the heart, you won't win the sale. Creating understanding is the key to winning the heart.

The very best way to cause understanding, one that's even better than an illustration or story (as good as they are), is by getting the listener to actually try and do what you are teaching them. Remember how Jesus sent out the disciples to go and "do" the same things He said and did?

That worked out pretty well.

The very definition of the Greek word used for "understanding" in the parable of the sower means ***"the coming together of the perception with the thing being perceived."*** In other words, it's where theory meets practice. When that happens, you've got it!

You can watch videos about learning to ride a bike all day long, but until theory meets practice, you will never truly know how to ride a bike. You will only know in theory. To the extent you can get your prospects to experience what you have to offer, where the thing you've been telling them about is the thing they are now experiencing, is the extent to which you will gain buy-in.

It's like the first time you heard about the iPhone, and how with your finger, you could scroll down the screen. It was one thing to hear about it and rationally understand the feature being described, but seeing it in action, and better yet, trying it yourself, usually sealed the deal… Because you truly understood.

I don't know what it's like to be in a fire fight in LIVE combat with a mortal enemy who is trying to kill you. I've read about it. I've seen many movies with scenes like that. I've even seen actual footage of real gunfights and saw real men, fall dead. But I know that I have no idea of what it's really like to be in that situation. I have no understanding. Only left-brain data.

Men who have been through battles together... They understand. And they know that others will not, indeed cannot. Their heart and soul have been indelibly impacted by things too hard to describe, and impossible to forget, try as they may.

Admittedly, a gun fight in Iraq is a lot more dramatic than what you may be facing now, but it still makes the point, that if you impact the heart, your message will not be forgotten. If it was a favorable impact, that elicited desire for your product or sale, they will find a way to obtain whatever you're selling.

As you read through this book, you will find lots more on winning the heart to make sales, and how in combination with wisdom (the principal thing) it greatly multiplies your chances of making sales.

I close this chapter with the words of Solomon... *"Wisdom is the principal thing; Therefore get wisdom. And **in all your getting, get understanding.**"* (Proverbs 4:7)

CHAPTER 17

MERCY AND TRUTH – The Unfair Advantage

"Let not mercy and truth forsake you; Bind them around your neck, Write them on the tablet of your heart, **And so find favor** *and high esteem in the sight of God and man."* (Proverbs 3:3-4)

"All **the paths of the Lord are mercy and truth**, *to such as keep His covenant and His testimonies."* (Psalm 25:10)

*"***Mercy and truth** *belong to those who devise good."* (Proverbs 14:22)

This one is huge.

When I moved to America, I got a job in January of 1986 selling copiers. I had done that in Canada for about six years in two different provinces, but it had been out of that business for about two years, and my last stint in Toronto was anything but successful.

On my first day, the VP told me that they expected no sales my first month because I had to learn the equipment and begin finding leads. By the second month, they expected two sales and they wanted me fully up to speed by the third month with four sales per month thereafter. That meant they wanted me to make six sales in my first 90 days.

In my two years with that company, I never saw anyone make six sales in their first 90 days, but that was the goal, nonetheless. He told me that I should close one out of every four or five copier demonstrations. The national average he said, was one out of four.

Later that day, it was obvious something was troubling me, and I was asked what it was. I explained that they were expecting me to sell one out of four. "What's the problem?" they asked.

I said that means they want me to accept a 75% failure rate! Then I reasoned, "What farmer plants four rows of corn and then prays to God that only one of them comes up?!"

I picked up my Bible and said, "I'm going to study this and find principles and strategies that I can deliberately apply to the sales process and instead of selling one out of four, I intend to sell one out of one!" Needless to say, they thought I was a tad unrealistic.

I began studying Proverbs and I quickly came across Proverbs 3:3, *"Let not mercy and truth forsake you. Bind them around your neck..."* Now hold on... How in the world do you tie or bind mercy and truth around your neck?

And then it continues... *"Write them on the tablet of your heart. And so find favor and high esteem in the sight of God and man."*

Think on that! Who wouldn't want God and other people to give them favor in the marketplace?!?!

So, was I supposed to actually tie mercy and truth around my neck? You see, this is where so many people lose it. This is where there's a disconnect.

They read verses like that and think, that's a nice verse, and move on to the next one. But they don't think it through, as to how they can apply it practically to their work or business.

Well, for me, as I began to think about that, I thought, mercy meant that I was never going to try to get somebody to purchase from me (and maybe use my persuasion skills or strong arm them to close a sale) when it's not in their best interest.

I determined that I would only attempt to make a sale to someone when I believed it was in their best interest. That's merciful. The fact that you can get somebody to say yes, doesn't make it right. The merciful thing is to do what is right for someone.

And the second thing is truth. Telling the truth is more than just not telling a lie. In fact, lying, by definition, is "the intent to deceive". You can tell the truth selectively, leaving out critical details, and deceive someone. People sometimes hide behind the fact that the words they spoke were true, but if it led someone to believe a lie, it's still a lie.

So, I reported for duty the next day at the branch office where I was going to be working and my boss said, "Son, what are your goals?" And I said, "Well, you know sir, I've thought about it and my goal is to sell one out of one".

He looked at me like he had made the worst hiring decision of his career. He didn't think I showed signs of insanity during the interview process, but now suddenly he learned that I thought I was going to sell one out of one.

He laughed and thought that if I had said that in the interview, he never would have hired me, but they had already printed my business cards, so he decided to see what I could do.

I went to work and as it turned out, 90 days later, after diligently and consciously applying Proverbs 3 (and other Scriptures) to my daily activities, it was time for our quarterly review. I actually started mid-January and it was now mid-April, and time for our first quarter review.

When it came my turn to project my results on the screen stating the number of calls, demonstrations, sales, and revenue I had generated, I said, "I've been here 90 days. I've done 22 copier demonstrations, but I'm pleased to report to you that I also have 22 sales." That was one out of one and it was three and a half times a number that I had never seen anyone achieve.

How did that happen? I wasn't some slick, highly polished, smooth talking, salesman using pressure and manipulation. I simply, deliberately, and consciously applied mercy and truth to my daily activities, and I found favor in the sight of God and man.

Yes, skills are important, and you will learn a lot more in this book but applying mercy and truth in the marketplace was a game-changer for me. I believe it will be for you as well.

CHAPTER 18

Imagination – The GOD Card

"And the Lord said, Behold, the people is one, and they have all one language; and this they begin to do: and now nothing will be restrained from them, **which they have imagined to do**.*"* (Genesis 11:6 KJV)

"Perfect, absolute peace surrounds those **whose imaginations are consumed with You**; *they confidently trust in You."* (Isaiah 26:3 TPT)

"Now to him who is able to do immeasurably more than all **we ask or imagine**, *according to his power that is at work within us,"* (Eph. 3:20)

When God gave us imagination, He gave us a piece of Himself, of His Divine Nature. We are His children and thus according to Genesis 1:26 we were made in His image and in His LIKENESS.

No other creature under Heaven has the creative gift of imagination. That's why they are called "creatures", and we are called His children.

We were made just a little lower than Elohim (another name for God) (Psalm 8:5), but we are too afraid to say that, so we use the translation that says we are a little lower than the angels. But according to Hebrews 1:14, angels are ministering spirits sent forth to minister to us, not the other way around. In fact, we have what angels desire to look into. (1 Peter 1:12).

Didn't Jesus in John 10:34 quote Psalm 82:6 which says, *"You are gods, and all of you are children of the most High"*? Why do we shrink back from His Words? Are we too ashamed? Do we know ourselves better than God does? Do we remember the Genesis account better than He?

To be clear, we are NOT GOD, but we ARE His children, made in His image and likeness. From that, we should never shrink back. We can do nothing in and of ourselves, but He lives in us and operates through us and there is no limit to what He can accomplish through the life of one fully submitted to Him.

And when man fell in the garden, Jesus paid too dear a price for you and me to trivialize and count as nothing the full gift of restoration He made available to us.

Look what Jesus says to you and me… in John 14:20, 21, 23… *"I am in My Father, and you in Me, and I in you… And he who loves Me will be loved by My Father, and I will love him and manifest Myself to him… If anyone loves Me, he will keep My word; and My Father will love him, and We will come to him and make Our home with him."*

These words were not spoken to cattle or angels or any other created thing. They were spoken to YOU and to ME. Paul speaks of this amazing gift of Christ living in us, calling it a mystery and our hope of glory. (Colossians 1:27)

We have been given the mind of Christ (1 Corinthians 2:16) and have the capacity to think along the lines He does. And part of that God-like capacity is the gift of imagination.

With it you can do good or evil. Choose good. With your imagination you can construct your world. You can actually frame it from the ground up and in the process, learn by seeing exactly what to do in the physical realm.

According to the Brown-Driver-Briggs Hebrew Lexicon, the Hebrew word yêtser means "imagination that forms and frames up". It is your imagination that frames your reality.

All things are twice created. First in the imagination and then in the physical realm. Your imagination creates the framework with which to build. It allows you to see or envision the end result before you produce it.

You can use your imagination in a directed way to solve problems. You can accomplish more in a couple of hours, laying on the couch or walking in the woods, etc., imagining every detail of something you wish to create or any problem you wish to solve.

The solution you see, must be something you can believe. A vain imagination is a waste of time. It's one thing to imagine yourself being successful in some walk of life, but what exactly does that look like?

A very popular but seriously misguided book for decades has taught that if you imagine yourself being wealthy, it will happen. Well first of all, that is a most shallow goal, and the Bible says when you chase riches, they take wings and fly away. (Proverbs 23:5). It also says, *"the **love of money** is the root of all evil"*. (1 Timothy 6:10)

So don't waste your time in pursuit of provision that Jesus Himself promised would be provided when you seek first His kingdom and righteousness. (Matthew 6:33). Use your imagination to envision the company you can build that glorifies Him, that enriches the lives of everyone it touches.

What does that look like in exacting detail? Spend time imagining the products or services you will either create or represent. Imagine delivering the highest level of service, or perhaps the most efficient, or even some combination of the two.

Get into exacting detail. If your service would be the best, what would make it the best? How will you deliver that? What would it cost in terms of staff or supplies, etc.? See it all the way through.

Imagine how you would go to market with the innovation or dream that God is giving you the ability to see and to accomplish. Call to mind King David's prayer to make those meditations well pleasing to God.

A caveat: Sometimes you can't see all the way through. The children of Israel could not possibly see how they would escape Pharaoh who had them backed up to the Red Sea.

But God.

Abram didn't know the land he was headed to when he left Haran, but He trusted that God would show him as he went.

See yourself as a master craftsman who uses the incredible gift and power of imagination in a God directed way to bring about realities that shape our world and influence our culture while providing exceedingly well for our family, and good causes that God would have us support.

The challenge
I don't know about you, but when I spend time "Imagineering", my mind often wanders way off track. One

thing I have found extremely useful to arrest my thoughts when they get off track is to speak. I learned it from James 3:4-5... *"Look also at ships: although they are so large and are driven by fierce winds, they are turned by a very small rudder wherever the pilot desires.* **Even so the tongue***..."*

Your tongue (the words you speak) direct your path in life much like a rudder directs the path of a ship. You see, it's very difficult to speak about one thing while thinking about another. So, choose to speak out loud along the lines of your intended purpose and your imaginations will quickly fall in line. Your words can be the whip that keeps your mind and imagination stayed on the right course of the desired purpose.

But really, it's a cycle...
Your words keep your imagination focused and your imagination, when it becomes real within you, (when it drips down into your heart until it affects your emotions) fills up with an abundance from which the heart then again speaks. (Luke 6:45)

It's a process like making a cake.
You speak (add ingredients), think (mix them together, stir them up), then taste test and if necessary, speak (add more ingredients) and think some more (mix it altogether) until finally you have the right consistency.

Then comes the fiery trial… You put it the oven. You put your idea under the heat of scrutiny and testing until baked perfectly. Don't overly scrutinize so that you leave it in the oven too long. Take it out while it's still moist. Don't let it die in the paralysis of analysis. When baked just right, pull it out of the oven, dress it up (put icing on it) and take it market.

Sadly, but not surprisingly (given the subtlety of our adversary), many today have denied themselves the beauty and power of a God-created imagination that each of us possess. It is incumbent upon us to consecrate it to the Lord, for His glory. As King David said, *"Let the words of my mouth **and the meditation of my heart** be acceptable in your sight oh Lord, my strength and my redeemer."* (Psalm 19:14)

I took that verse and more fully amplified it from the implied meanings in the original Hebrew. It reads like this…

"Let the words of my mouth, the speeches I give, the messages I deliver and the meditations, musings, even the very ponderings and resounding music I hear within my midst (my inner being) and dance within my heart, bring delight and satisfaction to you oh LORD my strength, my beautiful rock, my Mighty One and my redeemer, who purchased me from destruction and delivered me from slavery."

The person who can harness at will, the gift of directed imagination towards a desired end result, in a way that is as vivid as anything seen in the created order, and so real to them as to impact their emotions in a tangible expression, be that a smile, a laugh, a tear or a joyful sense of expectation, will by definition have proceeded through hope unto faith and with that faith will certainly apprehend the object of their desire.

In closing, I offer these words of Jesus. Let them speak to you… *"If you can believe, **all things are possible to him who believes.**"* (Mark 9:23) *"Have faith in God. (Have the faith of God) For assuredly, I say to you, whoever says to this mountain, 'Be removed and be cast into the sea,' and does not doubt in his heart, **but believes that those things he says will be done**, he will have whatever he says. Therefore, I say to you, whatever things you ask when you pray, **believe that you receive them, and you will have them**."* (Mark 11:22-24)

CHAPTER 19

Problems Are Your Provision

"Elisha replied, 'Hear the word of the Lord. This is what the Lord says: About this time tomorrow, a seah of the finest flour will sell for a shekel and two seahs of barley for a shekel at the gate of Samaria.' Then **the people went out and plundered the tents of the Syrians**. *So a seah of fine flour was sold for a shekel, and two seahs of barley for a shekel, according to the word of the Lord."* (2 Kings 7:1, 16)

If you've got problems, I've got great news. Your problems are guarding your provision because opportunity and adversity are joined at the hip. They are as inseparable as a shadow being cast by a tree in the sun. Let me recap a story in the Bible that really makes the point.

About 830 years before Christ, a prophet named Elisha was living in Samaria and their city was besieged by the Syrians. As food ran out, a donkey's head was selling as food for $400 or $500 in today's money and a cup of dove dung was selling for $25 or $30. It got so bad that women were killing and boiling their own children.

That's about as desperate as it gets.

It was in that circumstance that Elisha received a word from the Lord that the very next day things would turn around so much that you would be able to buy the equivalent of a pound of fine flour for about 70 cents.

No one believed him. And you might not believe what I'm about to tell you after you read this story, but it's still true.

As it turned out, there were four lepers just outside the city gates who were also starving. They reasoned that if they went inside the city gates, they would starve to death with everyone else, but if they stayed just outside the city walls, they would also starve.

So that night, they elected to surrender to the Syrian army. As they approached the enemy's camp, the Lord caused the Syrians to hear the noise of a great army approaching. It was so terrifying that the army ran for their lives, leaving everything behind, including their silver and gold, their horses and mules and all of their abundant food provisions.

When the four lepers got to the camp, they couldn't believe their good fortune. After grabbing a bite to eat and filling their pockets with silver and gold, they decided to go back to the city and report this incredibly good news to the guards at the gate.

Once the report was verified, the people inside the city rushed out the city gates and plundered the Syrian camp. When daybreak came, you could buy a pound of fine flour for about 70 cents just like Elisha had said.

The Israelites had been starving because they refused to confront the source of their problem, the Syrian army. The four lepers recognized the source of their problem and decided they had nothing to lose by going towards it.

They reasoned that if they stayed there or inside the city, they would starve to death with everyone else, so they might as well go in the direction of the problem in case there was provision there. Worst case scenario, they would die at the hands of the Syrians, which was no worse than their current options.

With the fear of losing out of the way...
They were able to walk right up to their massive problem (the Syrian army) and God caused the problem to flee in terror. But it didn't happen until they took action. The rest of Israel was too afraid to confront their problem and they would have died had it not been for a few men with nothing to lose.

What did the lepers find when they got there? They found the promise of Psalm 23, that the Lord had prepared a table right there in front of them, in the midst of their enemies!

Don't let the fear of losing keep you back from your provision.
So many people are afraid of losing that they never venture out of the security of what they know. And slowly, very slowly, they die on the inside. First their dreams die. Then their hopes. Then their joy. And then one day, they die, having lived a life of smallness of heart and mediocrity at best.

Listen... Problems are your provision. They stand guard over great opportunities, ready to turn them over to anyone willing to harvest them. So why does God allow problems to surround your provision? Because...

> "THE WISDOM YOU NEED TO CONQUER THE PROBLEM IS THE WISDOM YOU NEED TO STEWARD THE REWARD."

This is borne out by the vast majority of lottery winners who end up broke in just a few years because they never acquired the wisdom to steward the prize they won.

Don't let the fear of loss keep you at arm's length from the opportunity God has put in front of you. Problems are everywhere. That's good news because it makes it easy to see where the opportunity and provision are stored for you.

The provision is always joined at the hip with a problem to solve. It's just waiting for the brave, the courageous, the willing, to come and dine on the feast prepared in the midst of their enemies. But most people avoid or even run from their problems. In doing so, they are also running away from their provision.

Go towards your problem. Don't let fear of loss hold you back from your provision. It is always present in the midst of your problems. Let me paraphrase the words of Jesus in Luke 17:33 *"Whoever seeks to save his life by avoiding problems will lose it, and whoever is willing to lose his life in the act of confronting problems will in fact, preserve it."*

That's what the four lepers did. Why not us?

CHAPTER 20

The Bigger Your Problem, The Bigger Your Opportunity!

*"Only do not rebel against the Lord, neither fear the people (giants) of the land, for **they are bread for us**. Their defense and the shadow [of protection] is removed from over them, but the Lord is with us. Fear them not."* (Numbers 14:9)

*"Give us this day, **our daily bread**..."* (Matthew 6:12)

Problems are your food source.
The challenges and difficulties you face in life, are your food source. If you don't eat food, you will get weak and die. If you eat food, it will sustain you. The same is true with problems, challenges, and adversities.

They're a means of supply for you. They serve to develop your strength. If you don't face your problems and devour them, you'll grow weak and die. If not naturally, then internally.

Victory is sweet, but impossible without a problem, challenge, or adversity to overcome. When problems come, REJOICE! They ALWAYS contain the solution. They ALWAYS contain your provision. They ALWAYS lead to something equal to, or better than, the problem itself.

If you want the problem to persist, just avoid it. Don't face it or look at it. That way, you can guarantee it will hang around and even grow bigger.

Some problems are like milk. Others like bread. Some like meat. Every problem, every challenge, every adversity coming at you, is a bundle, a package of opportunity and provision.

People complain about lack. Are you kidding me? They are waist deep in problems, which means they are waist deep in opportunity. The opportunities look like problems, BECAUSE THEY ARE, and it's in the solving of the problem, they find their food.

Cracking the problem code, makes you strong and prosperous. The problems, challenges, and adversities are in fact, the way. Quit trying to avoid problems. Look for them. Solve them and grow rich in the process.

More people become millionaires by solving problems than by any other means. Be a problem solver and the world will become your oyster. (Remember, it's that problematic grain of sand inside the oyster that produces the pearl of great price!)

Joshua and Caleb came back from scouting out the Promised Land and concluded that the giants were actually their pathway to provision. The cities were built. The fields were plowed. The land was fertile. It was an incredible opportunity, but it was guarded by problems, as opportunities always are.

The people were too intimidated by the problem of the giants, so they slowly died out where they were. Close enough to see the promise but too afraid to claim it. Not true of Joshua and Caleb who 40 years later, when the naysayers had died out, entered the land, and took a great possession.

When David centuries later looked upon Goliath (another giant), he realized he had come upon the opportunity of a lifetime. An opportunity that promised great riches (wealth), the king's daughter in marriage (position) and tax-free living (privilege). He was so excited and confident in his viewpoint that he literally ran towards the problem giant, killed him, and claimed his reward.

Jesus faced the crucifixion head on
For the joy that was set before Him, Jesus endured the cross, despising the shame and in the end, sat down at the right hand of the throne of God. (Hebrews 12:2)

Every great advancement in my life came by overcoming a problem. Some of them were existential threats to my business but I knew that those threats were only going to destroy my business if I let them. But if I faced the problem and attacked it, the provision came to me in heaps!

This happened too many times to recount here and now, but one time I recall was when we were publishing my first book, ***The Bible Incorporated – In Your Life, Job & Business***. We were in our 2nd print run of 25,000 books.

The only way we could pay for these books was to pre-sell thousands which we had done. However, on the day of the printing, our largest customer canceled their order of 5000 books, which meant we had no way of paying for the print run. I knew it was an existential threat to our business and I knew that it must contain an equal or greater opportunity.

I just needed to see it.
I asked God for His solution and within minutes the solution became apparent. Instead of publishing 25,000 leather bound books, we would do 5,000 leather bound and 20,000 paperbacks.

That was a novel idea to us, but the paperback version went on to become our best seller and highly profitable! The problem ALWAYS has an abundance of provision!

How do you solve problems?
The short answer is to face them. See them as opportunities. The bigger the problem, the bigger the opportunity. It's a spiritual law that is beyond contestation!

Ask God for His wisdom and the best strategy or response to unlock the provision contained inside the problem. He will do that. For me, that sometimes comes in that still small voice, but it often comes out of me as I begin to discuss possible solutions

Where are the problems facing you now? Go looking for the problem you can solve, especially the problems other people are facing and don't know how to solve. You look at the path in front of you and it is strewn with problems, challenges, and adversity. Rejoice! They ALL contain provision!

Quit chasing riches! Proverbs 23:4-5 says: *"Do not overwork to be rich; Because of your own understanding, cease! Will you set your eyes on that which is not? For riches certainly make themselves wings; They fly away like an eagle toward heaven."*

Instead, chase down problems. Become great at solving them. They contain your provision. You never find money in a sack at the side of the road. If you do, it belongs to someone else. You find provision joined at the hip to the problem. Chase the problem down and take the reward attached to it.

In summary
The greater the adversity, the greater the opportunity. When you find yourself in the grip of adversity, *"count it all joy knowing this, that the trying of your faith works patience. But let patience have her perfect work, that you may be perfect and entire,* **lacking in nothing**.*"* (James 1:4) The end result of adversity can be sweet fruit indeed!

Be purposeful. Look for the opportunity. Ask God to show you the potential reward. Those who solve problems are of high value to any society and oftentimes that value even has a financial benefit to it.

When you get good at solving problems, look for others who have problems and ask God for how to solve their problems. That's what good businesses do. They solve problems other people can't or won't. When you do that well, adversity can be a most lucrative opportunity for you. Count it all joy.

It's your inheritance. Do it now.

CHAPTER 21

The Lies We Believe Are What Hold Us Back

"There we saw the giants (the descendants of Anak came from the giants); and we were like grasshoppers in our own sight, **and so we were in their sight***.”* (Numbers 13:33)

"And you shall know the truth **and the truth shall set you free***.”* (John 8:32)

All of us believe lies. If we knew which of the things we believed that were in fact false, we would stop believing them – or so you would hope. There are lies about ourselves, our worth, our potential, our problems, our past, etc., that we believe, but are not true.

You can stunt your potential…
What's so insidious about the lies, besides the fact that we can't see them, is that they are deeply embedded in our heart. At an intellectual level we may well disavow those lies and say we don't believe them and be sincere, but if you want to know what you really believe, pay attention to what you do.

It's the action that tells the story. Sometimes the lie is so deeply embedded it has become part of us and we don't realize it. As a result, we stunt our potential.

For example, when I was 11 years old, my father and stepmother divorced. It was decided I would be better off with my stepmother and her 3 older children. I didn't feel particularly attached to my new setting and got in trouble with the law, so I decided to run away and live on the streets of Toronto.

I was only gone a few hours when I was picked up and brought back home. My stepmom decided I wasn't worth the trouble and dropped me off at my grandmother's apartment on a Friday, promising to pick me up on Monday. The thing was though… she had no intention of coming back for me. And didn't.

My father had moved to Perth, Australia, but when he heard about the situation, moved back to Canada and my life took on some normalcy, graduating high school early, and was on my own at age 18, while my dad and his wife moved 4000 miles away.

After I got married years later, I was often asked if I ever felt rejected from that experience or from an earlier time at age 3 when I was dropped off at a stranger's house and never saw my real mother again. My answer was always the same… No. I was fine. I honestly felt no animosity or resentment for being lied to and dumped at age 11.

But then something happened when I was 37. My Dad wrote me a letter and mentioned that my stepmom had died and thought I would want to know. When I read those words, a bomb went off inside me. As fiercely as you can imagine, in a knee-jerk reaction on the inside, I said, *"**GOOD!**"*

It was at that moment that I discovered that deep down inside me, I deeply resented being discarded at age 11, and the object of my previously unknown resentment was my stepmom. At age 37, sitting on the sofa, tears ran down my cheeks in uncontrollable sobs. I had no idea that was inside of me!

Fortunately, I was able to release that resentment and forgive her right away. I knew better than to consciously hold on to it.

But for 26 years I had believed that I did not feel rejection and I had no resentment. Truth was that I did, but it was buried so deeply, I really didn't know. How much that buried resentment affected my relationships, I do not know, but when I let go of it, there was a great sense of relief!

Lies we believe even in an unconscious way, hold us back in much the same way elephants are held back in the circus. When baby elephants are brought into the circus, a small rope is tied around their leg at one end and fastened to a stake or pole at the other to keep them from running away.

As the elephant grows up however, eventually weighing several tons, they can easily pull away from the stake and go free.

The thing is though… they don't.
They grew up believing the rope defined their freedom or lack thereof and as an adult elephant, as soon as they feel the tug of the rope, they give in. They accept the limits of the rope even though they no longer apply. What they believe about the rope and its strength to hold them back, is a lie.

In a similar way, the lies we believe, define what we believe about our potential, and it goes undeveloped. No doubt I was held back by an invisible rope with no strength, but I was so used to living with that sense of rejection, I submitted to its limitations and found myself striving for the acceptance I never had as a child.

Ask those closest to you to speak truth to you, to help you expose the lies you believe and to affirm the truth they see in you. Don't be defensive.

Ask them for what they see to be your strengths, possibilities, and potential along with your weaknesses. Ask them what they think holds you back.

Make it safe for them to tell you the truth and they will. The truth may be uncomfortable at first, but it will set you free and lead you to fruitfulness.

Don't fear the truth because when you know the truth, it will set you free! (John 8:32)

CHAPTER 22

Seven Wealth Building Secrets of Isaac

"There was a famine in the land… **Then Isaac sowed** *in the land, and reaped in the same year, a hundredfold."* (Genesis 26:1, 12)

I want to share with you seven key secrets to Isaac's great wealth that may not only unlock success for you, but also possibly reveal while success has eluded you to some extent.

It all begins with his upbringing. By the time Isaac was born, Abraham was about 100 years old, and he lived for another 75 years! Think of all the mistakes you may have made raising your kids, that you wouldn't make now if you're in your later years. I believe all of us would make much better parents later in life, assuming we had the health and vitality to go along with it.

Secret # 1 – Character

Paul tells young people in Ephesians 6:2-3 to *"Honor your father and mother, which is the first commandment with promise: that it **may be well*** *with you, and you may live long on the earth."* The phrase "may be well" literally means "to be well off, fare well, prosper".

Consider this… When Isaac was a lad, perhaps about 10 - 12 years of age, his father Abraham took him on a three-day journey to go and worship. Most Christians in North America drive to church in less than 30 minutes where they intend to worship God. There is no record of Isaac complaining that he had to walk for three days just to get to the place of worship.

But that respect for his father goes much further because Isaac gets a little concerned that they've gotten to the place of worship, and they had no lamb for the offering. When he points this out to his father, he is reassured that God will provide Himself a lamb. (Genesis 22:8)

But imagine the next scene... Abraham takes some rope and binds his son and lays him on the altar with the wood. I think most kids would have run the other direction, but Isaac apparently offered no resistance.

We all recognize the faith of Abraham and rightly so, but let's not minimize the willing cooperation of Isaac, who responded to his father's instructions in similar fashion to how Jesus responded to His Father's will... "Not my will, but yours".

I would argue that showed incredible character in Isaac, even as a child that would serve him well for the rest of his life. His character shone through in his love for his wife and his interactions and conflict resolution skills later in life.

Secret # 2 – Let God Plant You
When famine came to Isaac, he was going to do what his father Abraham did years earlier in the previous famine, and head to Egypt where there was no famine, but God intervened and said, *"Do not go down to Egypt; live in the land of which I shall tell you. Dwell in this land, and I will be with you and bless you; for to you and your descendants I give all these lands, and I will perform the oath which I swore to Abraham your father."* (Genesis 26:2-3)

Let God plant you where He wants to plant you. He will bless you there in ways that won't happen elsewhere. Big doors turn on small hinges. If your business is location dependent (i.e., retail), seek God's direction for where to locate. If it is customer specific, ask Him where to find those customers. He may direct you to places or advertising venues you've never considered.

This even applies to your job. Be sensitive to when God may speak to you about where to work or whom to work for. I believe God gives us lots of latitude in these decisions and is often guiding us when we don't even know it. But what I'm referring to here is being sensitive to the leading of the Spirit.

As I discuss in more detail on the chapter about defeating the giants in your life, when I first moved to Nashville, TN, I wanted to make a mark in this world and do something epic for God. I considered several things and had many options. There was really only one thing I knew for sure that I didn't want to do… Sell copiers again!

But as I was driving west on I-40 through the downtown area of Nashville, the Holy Spirit drew my eye to a building and said, *"That's where you're going to work."* I had no idea what kind of business it was, nor was I looking for a place of employment that day.

It was a copier dealer, and I reluctantly went there to apply for a job that resulted in a dramatic turnaround in my life, and great success. However, it wasn't without some trials and tribulation, which brings me to a related matter… If God leads you to a job or responsibility, you don't leave until He leads you out.

About ten months after I was promoted to sales manager, I tangled with the new Executive Vice President who among other things, on his first day, explicitly told me not to mix "religion and business". One day he and I came to within a hairs breadth of coming to blows. I'll tell you the story sometime, but suffice it to say, I wanted to leave, and those who knew me, strongly encouraged me to do so.

But I figured, if God led me there, I should stay until He made it clear for me to leave, and not just leave because it got very uncomfortable. So, here's what happened…

One day, I set up a meeting with one of my salesmen to meet at the office at 2 PM. I was there on time, but he didn't show. As the hours passed, I got a little steamed, but waited to hear what his reason was.

When he finally sauntered into the office just after 5 PM, I asked him if he forgot the appointment or if he got tied up with a customer? He assured me that he did not forget, nor was he with a customer… he was just out driving around his territory.

As I ushered him into my office, I was prepared to land pretty hard on him, when the Holy Spirit interrupted my thought process before we were seated and said, *"Mercy!"*

I said under my breath, "Mercy!!! He doesn't deserve mercy!" And instantly the Holy Spirit said, *"Neither did you, but before he leaves your office he will be born again, and then you are free to leave the company."*

Now I realize some of you reading this may not believe God actually speaks to people these days, but I heard that doctrine too late in life. I had already heard Him clearly more times that I can count.

I spoke kindly to the young man and asked him questions about his upbringing, schooling, and life in general. Long story short, I shared the gospel with him as well, and he wept, gave his life to Jesus, and when he showed up for work the next day, he had what I called, "Perma-grin" because he couldn't stop grinning and smiling. His life had totally changed. He was indeed a new creation in Christ. (2 Corinthians 5:17)

And then, I planned my exit and was gone in a matter of weeks. Imagine if I had left the company earlier when I was wronged because I was uncomfortable. Who knows what the fate of that young man I led to Christ would have been?

Secret # 3 – Sow in Times of Adversity and/or Uncertainty
"There was a famine in the land, besides the first famine that was in the days of Abraham. And Isaac went to Abimelech king of the Philistines, in Gerar... Then Isaac sowed in that land and reaped in the same year a hundredfold; and the LORD blessed him." (Genesis 26:1, 12)

Think about this for a minute. Isaac buys some grain, most likely wheat for about $100 in today's money. Maybe more because it was a time of famine. But then, instead of eating it, he buried it in the ground, when everyone else was eating theirs just to survive.

When harvest came, he may have been the only one with grain, and he had 100 times more than he planted. If you're the only one with grain and everyone's hungry, you can get a premium price for your wheat due to the basic law of supply and demand. He knew if he was right, prices would be high at harvest time.

I have a personal connection to the grain market. You see, about a hundred years ago, my great grandfather was considered by many to be the shrewdest and ablest grain man in Canada. He came closer than any man in history to cornering the wheat market.

My father told me that one day he went to lunch with him in the 1920's, and when they got back from lunch, he checked his account and had made $85,000 while gone to lunch. That would be about $1.4 million in 2022! He was a big wheel in the wheat business.

However, in 1929 there was great optimism that prices would rebound from the record wheat harvest in Canada which had driven prices lower: He was so bullish on prices that he decided not to hedge the grain that his companies were buying. Instead of rising, prices began to fall, creating huge losses for him, nearly driving him to bankruptcy.

Though the crash was devastating, he still managed to prosper through the depression, but not near the previous level.

Now, as I finish writing this book, there is talk daily on the news about the possibility of WW3. That's never happened in my lifetime, or yours! We're still dealing with COVID and the man sitting in the White House just got his 2nd booster shot. (To each his own.) And now that 99% of public schools are back in operation, Fauci just today, warned of more restrictions coming. I'd say we are definitely living in uncertain times!

Regardless of what our circumstances are, there are always people who go against the flow of fear and are willing to take risks. Sure, not every business will make it, but you can greatly improve the likelihood of your success by following the advice in this book.

More millionaires were made during the Great Depression than in any other similar period in American history. One story I particularly like that you may be somewhat familiar with, is that of Harland David Sanders, the general manager of a service station in 1924 that closed down during the depression in 1930.

The Shell Oil company gave him another location to run, rent free, just to keep their product flowing in a small community just south of Lexington, Kentucky. Sales were slow, so to improve his revenue, he started selling a food product that his friends had come to love and appreciate. You know that food by the name, KFC (Kentucky Fried Chicken). Colonel Sanders, as he was known, did pretty well for himself!

When others are pulling back, it's a fabulous time to advance. Isaac had seen God provide a lamb just as his father was poised to drive a knife through his heart. He knew he could trust God, much like his father did. And he knew that God could prosper him despite the famine, because He had promised to do so.

What has God promised you?
Paul said that all of God's promises are "yes" and "amen", (2 Corinthians 1:20) so our job is to take hold of His promises and say, "so be it" which is the meaning of the word, "amen". Then match our actions to our faith in His promises and launch out, despite the uncertainty of the times. As Solomon sagely wrote, *"He who observes the wind will not sow, and he who regards the clouds will not reap."* (Ecclesiastes 11:4)

Secret # 4 – He Was a Business Owner
I want you to notice the threefold progression for Isaac's prosperity… Genesis 26:13 reads, *"The man began to prosper"* …

(Level 1) *"and continued prospering"* … (Level 2) *"until he became very prosperous;"* (Level 3) (See the chapter on the Rule of Three for more insight.)

All of that unfolded when he was a business owner. Genesis 26:14 explains… *"for he had **possessions** of flocks and **possessions** of herds and a great number of servants."* When it says he had possessions (plural) that meant he was the owner, not some other employer.

Furthermore, it says he had a great number of servants, which in today's vernacular would be employees or contractors. It takes a special skill and maturity and risk to have lots of employees, but as Proverbs 14:4 says, *"Where no oxen are, the trough is clean; But much increase comes by the strength of an ox."* In other words, employees may be a challenge and even make a mess, but much increase can come through them. (See chapter on "Leverage Through Others".)

Of 472 millionaires that were surveyed in a scientific study published in Germany in 2012, only 11 of them built their wealth with stock investments. Approximately 47 of them became rich with real estate investments. The other 414 millionaires became rich as entrepreneurs.

A similar study done in the U.S. by Thomas Stanley revealed that of 733 millionaires, the majority became wealthy through their entrepreneurial endeavors.

Secret # 5 – He had Multiple Related Businesses
Isaac had three main endeavors most likely producing about 7 sources of cash flow for him, which is interesting because I just read today, that on average, millionaires have 7 income sources. Here's how I see Isaac's business success…

Revenue source # 1: It appears he started with agriculture. He apparently had access to some land he could work, and it required very little capital to buy a bushel of seed grain. In his first year, he got a 100-fold return. That would not only feed his family and perhaps his livestock, but most likely be a source of income by selling to the local population.

Suppose he started with ten bushels of wheat. In today's world that would be about a $100 investment. Not much to get started. An acre of wheat can produce about 40 bushels, so if he got a 100-fold return on ten bushels, it would have required 25 acres (10 hectares). His $100 investment would have yielded about $10,000 in marketable wheat. Basically, he invested like a bull – in a bear market!

Revenue source # 2, 3 and 4: Isaac had flocks, of which in that day, it was customary or normal to have both sheep and goats. Sheep provided wool for clothing. Goats provided milk for drinking, and both provided meat for roasting. Isaac didn't just have one for his family… he had multiple flocks of these animals. The wool, milk and meat would provide not only his family's needs but also likely be sold to the locals as well, providing multiple income streams.

Isaac could have spent $1,500 on ten ewe lambs (today's prices) and two years later potentially have 60 sheep. Sheering those sheep once a year would produce approximately seven to eight pounds of wool per sheep or 400 – 500 pounds of wool altogether.

Wool sells for about $2 a pound, so he could have recurring cash flow from 60 sheep of $1,000 per year just from the wool. Additionally, a sheep can produce about $400 per year of sheep milk which has no aftertaste and is high in cream content. With 60 sheep producing milk, that's another $24,000 per year.

Once the flocks got to the desired size, he could begin selling lambs for livestock at the rate of 120 lambs per year X $150. That's another $18,000 per year.

A good goat on the other hand, can produce 200 gallons of goat milk per year (or more) and sell for $15 per gallon (depending on where). That's another income stream of $3,000 per year X 60 goats = $180,000 per year. According to one of my students who raises goats near Wasilla, Alaska, the market price there is $18 per gallon.

Revenue source # 5, 6 & 7: Isaac had multiple herds of oxen. Not only would they have provided beef for the family, but also be sold in the marketplace. Additionally, some of the livestock would be sold for breeding so others could go into ranching if they so desired. And lastly, oxen were basically like tractors.

With the great number of servants and multiple herds of oxen that Isaac had, he may well have provided plowing services for poorer farmers who couldn't afford their own ox. Who knows, he might have even had a "used oxen lot" where folks could get a good deal on a late model ox.

Although I'm kidding about the oxen dealership, Solomon did make a lot of money trading horses that he imported from Egypt and sold to *"all the kings of the Hittites and the kings of Syria"* (1 Kings 10:28-29) so the idea of selling beasts of burden was by no means foreign.

Notice that all of Isaac's business were related which made them more profitable due to efficiencies you can get with similar enterprises. For example, taking care of the sheep, goats and oxen had a lot of similar requirements and expertise, and they all needed similar food, which most likely was provided in part by his agricultural enterprise.

I did have a client that owned a beauty salon, a transmission shop, and a medical imaging business, but that's a lot harder to manage than if they were in related fields where his expertise could really be honed to benefit the whole. However, you can have completely unrelated businesses and succeed. It's often just harder.

Secret # 6 – He Shut Down Strife and Contention
"Also Isaac's servants dug in the valley, and found a well of running water there, but the herdsmen of Gerar quarreled with Isaac's herdsmen, saying, "The water is ours." So he called the name of the well Esek, because they quarreled with him." (Genesis 26:19-20) Esek means "contention". Rather than keep contention, he let them have it.

"Then they dug another well, and they quarreled over that one also. So he called its name Sitnah." (Genesis 26:21) Sitnah means "strife". Rather than be in strife, he moved again. The lesson here is clear… Isaac knew he could prosper and be fruitful much easier and faster if he could settle disputes quickly and get away from strife and contention, even if it cost him, and was unjust.

"And he moved from there and dug another well, and they did not quarrel over it. So he called its name Rehoboth, because he said, 'For now the LORD has made room for us, and we shall be fruitful in the land.'" (Genesis 26:22) Rehoboth means "wide places or streets".

Rather than fight it out in court, Isaac settled with them quickly so he could get on with his mission and prosper. He was looking for a wide place where he could expand. He let the small-minded folks have their strife and contention while he focused on peace, productivity, and profit.

Isaac was a master at relationships as demonstrated by the enterprise he built in a time of history when that required cooperation from all around you for mutual protection and for business. He loved his wife dearly and lived 180 years, which was five years longer than his father, Abraham.

Secret # 7 – His Word Was His Bond.
When Isaac made a commitment, he kept it, even if it turned out later to be a mistake. Take for example the trickery of his youngest son, Jacob who came to him when he was old and had poor vision, pretending to be the older brother Esau. Jacob at his mother's direction, succeeded in tricking Isaac to pronouncing a blessing upon him that rightfully belonged to the first-born older brother, Esau.

When the scheme was uncovered, it was too late. Isaac had blessed Jacob instead of Esau. When Esau pleaded with his father, Isaac replied, *"Indeed I have made him your master, and all his brethren I have given to him as servants; with grain and wine I have sustained him."* (Genesis 27:37)

Isaac continued and could only say this to the grief-stricken Esau… *"Behold, your dwelling shall be of the fatness of the earth, and of the dew of heaven from above. By your sword you shall live, and you shall serve your brother; And it shall come to pass, when you become restless, that you shall break his yoke from your neck."* (Genesis 27:39-40)
Isaac lived his life by keeping his word and believed that the words he spoke could never be rescinded. He must have

thought that spoken words had power. (That's worth chewing on, don't you think?)

As is also true today, Isaac's success resulted in the envy of the Philistines around him. (Genesis 26:14). Typically, the folks who envy you and dislike you for your success, are upset because they are not willing to do what you did to succeed. They don't resent you for your success. They resent you because they feel it makes them look bad.

Finally, Abimelech said, *"Go away from us, for you are much mightier than we."* (Genesis 26:16) When you begin to prosper in a big way, it's not that you don't value where you came from, but many times, those who didn't grow with you, will reject you.

CHAPTER 23

Faith That Actually Works!

*"Behold the proud, His soul is not upright in him; But the just shall **live by his faith**."* (Habakkuk 2:4)

*"Now **the just shall live by faith**; But if anyone draws back, My soul has no pleasure in him."* (Hebrews 10:38)

This chapter could easily fill a book if I allowed myself the liberty and you afforded me the high honor of your attention for such a work. But that is not the full burden of this book, so I will confine my sharing to a few Scriptures and hopefully unscramble the egg of misunderstanding on this vital topic.

Have you ever heard of someone who perhaps was going to a faraway land to be a missionary and they had no visible means of support, so they said they were going to have "live by faith"?

Whenever I heard someone say something like that, I thought, "Oh my, it's come down to that. We need to start a prayer chain for these people! They're going to just live by faith. They have no job, no income, just faith. We better pray for them!"

In other words, the idea of someone "living by faith" was a scary proposition. Perhaps even an act of desperation or "last resort". But catch this…

Living By Faith Was Meant to Make Life *Easier*, NOT Harder!

So why does it seem so hard? I submit that we have very little understanding of what Jesus actually did for us. We cling (and rightly so) to salvation, but few go much further. We may sing about matters of faith and victory, but we rarely experience them. And when we do, we can't seem to replicate it on demand.

Even those of us with miracles in our experience tend to look at them through the rear-view mirror and even that sometimes requires binoculars because of the great passage of time since the last one occurred. It need not be that way.

Have you ever read this passage in John 16:23-24?

"And in that day you will ask Me nothing. Most assuredly, I say to you, whatever you ask the Father in My name He will give you. Until now you have asked nothing in My name. Ask, and you will receive, that your joy may be full."

When Jesus said, *"And in that day, you will ask Me nothing",* what day was He referring to? Jesus had just told His disciples in verse 16, *"A little while, and you will not see Me; and again, a little while, and you will see Me, because I go to the Father."*

Some contend that when Jesus said *"a little while, and you will see Me…"* He was referring to the space of time between when He would leave the planet physically and when He would return. But let's use a little sanctified common sense here…

It's been 2000 years so far… Does that seem like just a little while to you? I know a day is as a thousand years to the Lord, but He was answering the questions of some of his disciples who didn't understand what He meant that for "a little while" they would not see Him, but then "in a little while" they would.

Obviously when He said, *"a little while, and you will not see Me"*, that was fairly imminent as He knew He would soon be crucified and buried, and they would not see Him. But then He says *"and AGAIN a little while, and you will see Me."*

Jesus compared the temporary separation to the anguish of a woman giving birth, who after the delivery of the baby, would forget her anguish and rejoice.

The "day" Jesus was referring to was post resurrection, three days later. Can you imagine the anguish of seeing Him crucified and then, the unspeakable joy of seeing Him a few days later, resurrected and fully alive? That's what He was talking about.

Now follow this carefully… Do you know how in the Greek, there are three common words translated as "love" (eros, phileo and agape)? They have different meanings (erotic love, brotherly love and unconditional love) but they are all translated with one word, "love".

Well, it turns out the same is true about other words, and that's where there's a real eye opener. When Jesus says, *"And in that day you will **ask** me nothing"*, the word "ask" in the Greek is different from the word "ask" in the rest of the passage.

The first word "ask" is "erotao" in Greek and means to *"ask, beseech, intreat or beg"*. When He continues the thought He says, *"Most assuredly, I say to you, whatever you **ask** the Father in My name He will give you. Until now you have **asked** nothing in My name. **Ask**, and you will receive that your joy may be full."*

For the rest of the passage the Greek word translated as "ask" is "aiteo" which means to *"ask, desire, require, call for or put a demand on"*. Paraphrasing in modern vernacular, here is what Jesus was communicating…

> *"In just a few days, when My work on the cross is complete, everything changes for you. You won't need to beg or intreat Me for anything. No more feeling like you're a poor man asking for a loan at the bank. What I'm telling you, you can take to the bank alright, but it's a cashier's check with My name on the account. You can fill it out anyway you please and My Father who owns the bank, will give you whatever you put on it. No questions asked because I have pre-authorized the check.*
>
> *Until now, you didn't have My name to back up your requests, so you never put a demand on my infinite supply. You were more like a beggar asking for a loan than a person with a cashier's check in hand. From now on, ask for what you need in the same way you would ask a bank teller to cash a certified check from Me. That's not arrogant or demanding. It's a simple transaction based on an approved and authorized signature. So be confident when you approach the Father, knowing that your request has already been pre-approved, so that your joy may be full."*

In John 14:12-14, Jesus said, *"Most assuredly, I say to you, he who believes in Me, the works that I do, he will do also; and greater works than these he will do, because I go to My Father. And whatever you* **ask** *in My name, that I will do, that the Father may be glorified in the Son. If you* **ask** *anything in My name, I will do it."*

The word "**ask**" is "aiteo" again. It's the ask that you do when you know whatever you ask for has already been agreed to. I believe the reason we often don't experience that result is because we are approaching God as if Jesus never paid the price for us. We are still petitioning Him like the poor man asking for a meager loan.

Think of it another way if this helps. Two men go separately to a restaurant. When the first man arrives, his order has already been called in and paid for. He pulls up to the drive through window and asks for his order, confident that they will give him whatever he ordered.

The second man turns up at the restaurant. His food order was not pre-authorized. He has no means to pay for food, but he's hungry, so he humbly beseeches and entreats the owner for the favor of some food, not at all confident that the owner will oblige him.

They both asked, but the way they asked was quite different. One with complete faith that the meal, that was paid for, would be given to him upon request, and the other with a faint and perhaps desperate hope that maybe this time he might get something he needs. He asks even though he doubts his request will be granted.

Or think of it this way... You have a personal credit card with a $5,000 spending limit, but one day, you get hired by Apple Computers and are given a corporate American Express card – Platinum Level with no spending limit as a perk.

It used to be that you had to check your limit and get approval before spending, but now since you came in with an American Express Platinum level credit card in the name of Apple Computers, you can purchase whatever you want.

We are no longer lost and alone. We've been brought into the family of God and now can go in His name (Jesus), and nothing shall be impossible to us. You've probably heard about "the big reset" that's coming, well, we already had a big reset, and there will never be another one like it.

It's much more than a ticket to Heaven. It's how we can live our life in the NOW. You can still live your life according to the pre-reset days if you wish, but because of Calvary we are free to live in the new system, by faith, and experience the fulness of the true and living reset that took place 2000 years ago.

So, what does faith look like in business? The kind of faith that defies conventional wisdom. In the next chapter I'll give you one great example…

CHAPTER 24

All Things Are Possible
(Or Was Jesus Just Kidding?)

*"If you can believe, **all things are possible** to him who believes."* (Mark 9:23)

*"For assuredly, I say to you, whoever says to this mountain, 'Be removed and be cast into the sea,' and does not doubt in his heart, but believes that those things he says will be done, he will have whatever he says. Therefore, I say to you, **whatever things you ask when you pray, believe that you receive them, and you will have them**."* (Mark 11:23-24)

When I first started selling copiers in Nashville, I asked God to help me arrive at a good goal for my first full month in sales. I wanted it to be high enough to grab my employer's attention but within range of what I could believe was possible.

I know *"all things are possible"*, but there is a caveat… It says, *"to him who believes."* In theory, I believe I can walk on water, but in practice, I'm just not there yet. Make sense?

On my first day on the job, the VP of sales told me that they expected no sales my first month, two my second month, and only four per month once I got up and running.

I wanted to be a witness for Jesus on the job and I had learned that people tend to listen to and respect people who are successful, especially those who are successful in an area where they themselves are struggling.

I thought making ten sales in my first full month which was nearly double what they expected in my first three months combined, might be a good attention getter, and give me a platform of credibility from which I could share my faith with others.

Bear in mind, that in the copier business, the average sales cycle from when a company started looking for a copier and when they finally decided on a purchase, was around 30 days. On the last day of the month, on the way in to work I had a blowout on my front tire. No big deal, but it did delay my arrival by a couple of hours getting into the office.

When I arrived, I already had eight sales under my belt for the month with one sale I was hoping to close that day.

Unfortunately, there was a message from that prospect telling me he had made his final decision and he not only didn't want to buy at this time, but he specifically requested that I don't call him back.

By 2:00 PM that afternoon, with only three hours remaining in the business day I still needed two more sales to reach my goal and I thought I would call someone to bring them up to speed on my progress.

When I mentioned that I still had to find two prospects in three hours and turn them into happy customers before the close of business, they began to "encourage" me by reminding me that I had already sold eight copiers that month and nobody had ever done that in their first month with that firm and I didn't need to put that kind of pressure on myself, etc.

I interrupted them mid-stream and informed them that I couldn't allow them to talk to me like that anymore. I couldn't allow their words to penetrate my heart. I still believed that somehow, I could sell two more copiers in the next three hours even though I didn't have any prospects.

I couldn't allow their well-meaning words of encouragement to cause me to relax my grip and focus on the goal. You see, when Jesus said, *"Believe that you **receive** them, and you will have them"*, you need to understand the Greek word for "receive" is "lambano" which means to *"take with the hand, lay hold of, to claim or procure for one's self"*.

It's not a passive act like you might "receive" letters at your address. It's more like when a teenager with her driver's license (but still living at home), asks to borrow the car for the evening. When the father says yes, the teenager eagerly snatches the keys from Dad's hand. She doesn't sit down meekly waiting for her father to walk over and place them in her hand.

The receiving is an aggressive, taking hold of the promise and not backing away or second guessing.

I wasn't about to back away and second guess the number of ten copier sales my first month, despite the fact that there were only three hours left in the day and I had no prospects. Those may have been good reasons to doubt I would reach the goal, but I couldn't afford to consider those reasons and settle for being satisfied with just the eight sales I had already closed.

I had to "consider not" (Romans 4:19) all the very sound and logical reasons that indicated how unreasonable it was to even think about reaching that goal.

But I wasn't into being reasonable. I believed God and I were jointly working on that goal, and I wasn't about to give up on it. That fat lady might have been warming up in the choir loft, but she hadn't stepped up to the microphone to sing yet!

I actually hung-up on them as nicely as I knew how and hoped they would understand. A few minutes later, a man driving by our office saw the sign on our building and pulled in to inquire about purchasing a used copier. In the nearly seven years that I had sold copiers in Canada, before coming to the States, I had NEVER had a walk-in customer. It just didn't happen.

This gentleman informed me that he wouldn't be buying for several months but wanted to get an idea of what the investment might be. After learning about his needs, I brought him over to a good used copier which he felt perfectly met his requirements, though it had over 300,000 copies on it.

I asked him if he would be interested in the exact same model for the exact same price but with only one tenth of the usage and he answered in the affirmative. I called the one prospect (a CPA) that had left me that message earlier in the day not to call him. (Sometimes you just have to take a chance.)

I told him that I had a customer in our office that wanted to buy the same kind of copier that he currently had, and I was wondering if he wanted me to have this customer make the check payable to him or to us.

Essentially, I was offering to sell his used copier for him at retail price, and he asked me to bring the buyer over. When we arrived, the customer I brought with me, agreed to purchase his copier, which of course left the CPA with none, so he purchased one from me on the spot.

Two sales in three hours. Call it a miracle. Call it a coincidence. Call it ingenuity. Call it what you want. I know it wouldn't have happened if I had considered the reasons why it shouldn't have happened.

At the time, I believed God looked down on the whole scene, honored my faith, maybe even smiled at my optimism, then out of His grace and kindness sent me the assistance I needed to reach the goal.

But as I've grown in my walk with God, I've come to understand that what really happened was just the natural, non-mystical way that faith actually works. You believe it in your heart – not merely intellectually.

You declare it with your words, not to convince yourself, but rather to release the potency of conviction (faith) into the earth realm from a heart that is fully convinced. Then you merely line up your actions according to your expectation.

There is no wavering, no halting between two opinions. No "hoping" that it will work out - only a knowing that it will.

CHAPTER 25

You Only Think You've Been Trusting God!

"The Lord is good, a stronghold in the day of trouble, and **He knows them that trust in Him***;"* (Nahum 1:7)

"The man that **makes his trust in the Lord***, not respecting the proud or turning aside to lies* **will be blessed***."* (Psalm 40:4)

"It is **better to trust in the Lord**
than put confidence in man." (Psalm 118:8)

What I am about to tell you in many ways resembles this story found in Luke 5:1 – 9… *"So it was, as the multitude pressed about Him to hear the word of God, that He stood by the Lake of Gennesaret, and saw two boats standing by the lake; but the fishermen had gone from them and were washing their nets. Then He got into one of the boats, which was Simon's, and asked him to put out a little from the land. And He sat down and taught the multitudes from the boat.*

When He had stopped speaking, He said to Simon, 'Launch out into the deep and let down your nets for a catch.' But Simon answered and said to Him, 'Master, we have toiled all night and caught nothing; nevertheless, at Your word I will let down the net.'

And when they had done this, they caught a great number of fish, and their net was breaking. So they signaled to their partners in the other boat to come and help them. And they came and filled both the boats, so that they began to sink. When Simon Peter saw it, he fell down at Jesus' knees, saying, 'Depart from me, for I am a sinful man, O Lord!' For he and all who were with him were astonished at the catch of fish which they had taken;"

Peter, James and John took a break from washing their nets and just listened to Jesus teach. Good thing they were partners instead of employees or they might have been fired for slacking off.

Then Jesus told them to go out to the deep water and expect a catch. They almost sunk two boats with the amount of fish they brought in. The only limit really was the size of their boats.

So fast forward to August 31, 1979… I had a goal to set a personal sales record and hopefully win a contest in the process. The contest was for three months ending on August 31st.

By August 1st, I had already achieved the sales quota for the three-month period, and I still had one month to go. The way our month-ends worked, we actually had five full weeks that month to sell, and my prospects for success looked very good at the beginning of the month.

Two weeks into the month however, things had changed, and I had not gotten any sales under my belt. As I prayed about it, the overwhelming sense I would get from the Lord was to simply trust Him, so I continued.

Two more weeks passed, and not only did I still not have any sales under my belt but every prospect I had for making a sale had evaporated into thin air.

The Lord was still saying to my spirit, "Trust Me." Our sales quota was four units per month or $22,000 in revenue and I had never had a zero month before, and I was getting nervous.

It was week five… Monday, Tuesday, Wednesday and Thursday all came and went in the last week of the month without any sales whatsoever.

On the eve of the last day of the sales contest where I had been hoping to shatter previous records, I was sitting on a zero month! To make matters worse, I had no one ready to close a sale. Just some long shot prospects from cold leads that hadn't purchased from me before.

Late that night, one of the salesmen with whom I was competing, offered to pray for me. We sat there in my office; my head bowed and as he prayed, something quite unusual happened.

It was like a video clip started playing in my mind. I can't remember what he prayed but I vividly remember the video clip, and in that clip, I saw myself standing in the shallow end of a swimming pool with Jesus beside me.

As the scene unfolded in my mind, it was like it was really happening and Jesus asked me if I wanted to be baptized? He suggested that if I wanted, I could stay under the water for sixty seconds while He baptized me, and He would supernaturally enable me to breathe while under water.

In this video clip or vision playing in my mind and resonating in my heart, I accepted His offer. After sixty seconds, in the vision, I emerged from the water, gasping, and breathing excitedly saying, "I did it! I did it!"

That's when I realized that although I was under water for sixty seconds, I had done it in my own strength. I never inhaled while under water. I had held my breath. The video clip helped me understand that although I said I trusted Him, in fact I was relying on my own strength and ability.

I didn't quite know what to do with that understanding but the next morning I took my list of calls and instead of being uptight about the outcome, I completely left the outcome to the Lord, and I just went along for the ride.

The first place I called on, told me I was lucky to catch them because they were leaving early for Labor Day weekend, but they would listen to what I had to say. They listened and they bought a copier.

The second person I called on told me the same thing and they listened and then purchased a copier. The third person I spoke with that day bought a copier and then the fourth. I had hit my monthly quota in my first four calls!

I called my boss who asked me how I was doing, and I told him that I was inhaling! I think he took me literally! (But I would explain later.)

The fifth, sixth and seventh company I called on all bought copiers. A major hospital in my territory called in out of the blue and gave a purchase order for my eighth sale that day.

The ninth, tenth, eleventh and twelfth prospect – in a row – all bought copiers that day.

At about 5:30 I came into the office with $56,000 worth of signed orders and checks only to find out there was a message from someone who wanted us to mail them a brochure for our new reduction copier.

I got back in my car and drove it over to them, as they were still at the office. An hour later I walked out with a $10,000 order bringing it to thirteen sales in a row for a total of $66,000 worth of business, which in itself was a three-month quota.

You need to understand that only 15% of the company reps would ever achieve $66,000 worth of business in a three-month period. I experienced it all in one day… from prospects that were not on my "hot list". They were either at the bottom of the barrel long shots or not even on my radar!

When I shared this story with my friend Wes Cantrell, former CEO of Lanier Worldwide, he agreed that it had to be the unofficial world record for the greatest number of individual copier sales in a single day in the history of copier sales!

I believe I experienced a little of what it must have felt like when Peter obeyed Jesus and went out to the deep (where risk meets opportunity) and let down his net for a catch and then caught the biggest haul of his career.

Clearly, it wasn't about Peter's fishing skills; it was about God's intervention in the affairs of individual men. For me, I knew it wasn't about my great selling skills or charming personality.

It was about God showing Himself strong to anyone who will trust Him for the outcome. Since then, I can truthfully say that I've had other stories, equally or more impressive, all of which happened when totally throwing my trust on Him where my previous limits were tossed aside, and I was stretched as I learned to trust Him for more.

Prior to that day, I thought I had been trusting Him, but on August 31st, 1979, I learned what trusting Him really felt like, and it is the most glorious, peaceful, and joyful experience.

I encourage you to step out of your comfort zone and trust Him and remember that *"He Who promised is faithful."* (Hebrews 10:23)

CHAPTER 26

Never Give Up
(Taking Back What's Been Stolen)

*"Pursue, for you shall surely overtake them
and without fail **recover all**."* (1 Samuel 30:8)

*"For **whatever is born of God overcomes the world**. And this is
the victory that has overcome the world—our faith."* (1 John 5:4)

*"But thanks be to God, who **gives us the victory**
through our Lord Jesus Christ."* (1 Corinthians 15:57)

*"Now thanks be to God who always
leads us in triumph in Christ"* (2 Corinthians 2:14)

I read a billboard once that said, "Success consists of getting up one more time than your knocked down." Paul certainly knew about that. He was given 39 stripes from whippings on five different occasions but continued on.

He was stoned and left for dead but was raised up and continued on with His purpose. He was imprisoned frequently and turned those occasions into revival meetings. He was shipwrecked, snake bit and in perils of robbers and countrymen. But nothing could or would knock Paul off his purpose. He was determined to finish his course.

In 1 Samuel 30 we read that while David and his men were away, the Amalekites attacked his village and took captive the women and children, as well as all their possessions. His men were contemplating stoning him because he was the leader when this horrible thing happened.

David asked the Lord if he should pursue them and was told, that he should (1) pursue (2) overtake and (3) without fail, recover all. He did exactly that.

Abraham's nephew Lot was also kidnapped so Abraham took 318 trained servants and recovered all. These and many other men and women in the Bible faced horrific challenges, the likes of which few living today have ever seen. In every case, they got back up, pursued, overtook the enemy, and recovered all.

We are not promised an easy path. I've had many hardships in life. I've lost two brothers to suicide, had three mothers growing up, buried my first-born child (a beautiful downs syndrome girl), lost my home and investments, buried my father and finally my wife of 24 years. But I can tell you as God is my witness, in every circumstance, He lifted me up, restored my hope and my joy, and let me know my work was not done yet.

If he can give me sheer joy in the midst of my trials and restore my hope (which He has done), He can and will do the same for you. As He one time told me, when I was agonizing over the heartache of my first child being handicapped with downs syndrome, "Read 2 Corinthians 4:17."

Not knowing what it said, I turned and read, *"For our light affliction,* **which is but for a moment,** *is working for us a far more exceeding and eternal weight of glory,"* Verse 18 continues, *"while we do not look at the things which are seen, but at the things which are not seen. For the* **things which are seen are temporary, but the things which are not seen are eternal.***"*

God let me know that whatever we are enduring is a light affliction which endures for just a mere moment, and will do a work in us, (if we let it), that far exceeds the cost it extracts from us.

Friend, I know you may very well be in a hard place. Maybe it's your own doing, maybe it's not. We all make mistakes and many times they are grievous. Paul used to hunt down Christians. David had his lover's husband killed. Moses killed a guy too. These are some heavy hitters in the Bible with a record, but they acknowledged their wrong, turned to God and He used them for His great glory. He'll do that for you.

But it's up to you to get back in the game. You gotta quit feeling sorry for yourself, licking your wounds, blaming the other guy, holding on to resentment, etc. Quit that. Or as Paul said in 1 Corinthians 16:13, *"Watch ye, stand fast in the faith, quit you like men, be strong."*

Let me tell you a story about the day my life turned around. I had lost my teenage marriage, my children, my business, every earthly possession, my sense of worth and I thought even my destiny was lost.

In the space of less than 24 months, I had hit rock bottom. There were other factors too painful to mention, but suffice it to say, I was definitely swimming in a pool of self-pity.

But God...
Then one cold and dreary winter day in Canada, while waking up on someone else's couch in their living room, I turned on the television and saw the popular Christian TV show, <u>The 700 Club</u> airing.

I was only half awake and even less interested, but suddenly as I watched the television, the image transformed and I saw myself being interviewed and I saw my name at the bottom of the screen, even though in reality, that was not happening!

I stared at the TV in disbelief and wonderment, then quickly shut it off and went for a walk in the rain. It was incomprehensible to me that I would ever be on TV, let alone interviewed on *The 700 Club*.

Who would ever want to hear from me? I had failed at life, lost my family and was dead broke and still owed hundreds of thousands of dollars with no known way of paying that back.

As I walked in the gloomy drizzle the West Coast is famous for, I found a ravine with a creek wandering through it. It was there that I told God just how bad life really was. I had quite a list of failures, disappointments, and heartbreaks.

After an hour, when I finished pouring out my grievances to Him, telling Him how absurd it was that I would ever be considered for an interview on *The 700 Club*, He asked me a question… *"Are you tired of feeling sorry for yourself?"*

I was stunned by the clarity of His voice and the message He had for me. I was hoping for a hug or some words of encouragement. Instead, He challenged me.

The only response I could come up with was to spend equal time praying for people worse off than me, (if there were any, I thought). So, for the next hour, I prayed for everyone I knew that was going through challenges.

After that I prayed for people, I knew must exist, but I didn't know, who were undoubtedly being challenged in their life. I prayed for missionaries in Africa and China. I prayed for inmates in jail. I prayed for the homeless. I prayed for any group of people I could think of that might be in need.

After about an hour, strangely enough, I felt much better, no longer depressed, and I asked God a question… "What about me… will I ever be ESTABLISHED again?"

Without missing a beat, He responded with a Bible verse, 2 Chronicles 7:17. Like you perhaps, I had no idea what that said or even if it was in the Bible. I ran out of the ravine to my car, pulled out my Bible and hurriedly read the passage…

*"**As for YOU**, if you walk before me faithfully as David your father did, and do all I command, and observe my decrees and laws,"* verse 18 continues… *'**I WILL ESTABLISH** your royal throne…'* I knew this was a promise to Solomon but what I understood the Lord to be saying to me was essentially, *"If you will follow after me and keep My Word, I will ESTABLISH you."*

I was stunned at the direct answer to my question, and I held my Bible up in the air in the rain and with tears in my eyes, told the Lord that I would study His Word and do what it says and tell everyone else about that, BUT if He didn't do what it says He would do for folks, then I couldn't and wouldn't tell anyone.

God wasn't finished with me yet and I'm pretty sure He's not finished with you either. God wants you to rise up and stay the course. Pursue your destiny. Don't let the devil or anyone else keep you from obtaining the prize of the high calling of God in Christ Jesus for you. (Philippians 3:14)

Determine here and now, to *"forget those things which are behind, and reach forward to those things which are before you"* (Philippians 3:13). Decide now that you will rise back up, knowing that it's always darkest before the dawn and that joy comes in the morning. God is not finished with you, nor have you finished running your course. So don't let up, shut up or give up until He takes you up.

There's an amazing finale to this story that is hard to believe but would be dishonest to leave out. I'll finish it in the next chapter…

CHAPTER 27

Miracle Restoration

*"He **restores my soul**; He leads me in the
paths of righteousness for His name's sake."* (Psalm 23:4)

"Restore to me the joy of Your salvation
and uphold me by Your generous Spirit." (Psalm 51:12)

Well, after I told God I would study His Word, learn His ways and tell everyone about them, as long as He did what His Word says He would do, I then told Him that I had an urgent financial need in the amount of $1000. From there, I went back to my friend's house, got cleaned up and drove about 30 miles to call on a prospect.

It was Friday and almost noon when I got there, and the man rebuffed me coldly. Having no more leads to work on, I walked to a nearby restaurant to have some lunch.

As I approached the restaurant, the Lord interrupted my thoughts and just said, *"No."* I remember stopping on the street and wondering why God would say not to go there. It made no sense to me. It wasn't some seedy bar. It was a respectable, Christian-owned, family restaurant.

So, I proceeded. Once again, He said, *"No."* I hesitated but continued, thinking I must be imagining this. When I put my hand on the door, His voice was quite loud and firm… *"NO!"*

So, I turned around, went back to my car, and decided to head back to the suburb near where I was staying. On the way, while driving across the mile long Port Mann Bridge crossing the mighty Fraser River, I jokingly asked God if He had any particular place, He wanted me to go?

To my surprise, He heard me, and answered! His reply was as swift as it was surprising. He simply said, "Chi Chi's". I knew the restaurant. It was a big box Mexican restaurant I had never been to. I told Him, I hated that kind of food, but He didn't change His mind, so I drove to Chi Chi's, wondering if I was really playing with a full deck in my head.

Upon my arrival, I discovered there was a long wait, so I went back to my car to leave and find another restaurant. He told me to stay and have lunch there. I was beginning to seriously doubt my sanity but figured I might as well follow this through to its end.

When I was finally seated, I discovered that I was across from Rick Osborne, an old friend, a prolific writer with a profound relationship with God. He was in a meeting with someone but asked if I could wait around because he really needed to talk with me.

I was happy to oblige and thought this was my $1000 commission opportunity. I was sure he was going to buy something from me to help with his tax liabilities. Boy, was I wrong! He had an income problem, not a tax problem.

Totally deflated and certain now that my $1000 request to God had fallen on deaf ears, I offered to spend the weekend helping Rick by writing up a proposal and contract for a publisher he was hoping to get a big deal with. I told him I had no plans for the weekend, and I was not asking for any remuneration. I just thought I could help him.

My first experience seeking God for wisdom in writing a contract… Over the weekend, God gave me clause after clause, and innovative ideas that I incorporated into his presentation for Monday morning. Long story short, he presented it and walked out of that meeting with a fat check and a great contract! Needless to say, he was thrilled with the outcome!

Meantime, I was still asking the Lord when I would get the desperately needed $1000. He told me that it would be replenished when I had completely run out of money, and not until. That was cutting it too close for my liking, but what choice did I have? Not only did I have no sales prospects but the time I spent helping my friend Rick was as a gift and not done for a fee.

Later that week, Rick asked me to meet him at their CPA's office related to this deal, so I did. It was about a thirty-mile drive, and I was low on gas and had no more cash and no credit cards.

I arrived a bit early, and my gas gauge was on empty, so I pulled into the gas station, counted my coins and with some embarrassment, purchased roughly $1.38 in gas, which was less than a single gallon of fuel. It didn't even move the needle.

After the meeting, Rick asked me to meet him at his place, roughly 30 miles back in the direction I came from. As I was driving there on fumes, I realized I had no money, no gas, no credit, and no prospects for income.

With tears in my eyes, I looked toward Heaven and loudly declared, "Today is pay day! You promised that when I ran out, You would replenish. I have no resources whatsoever left. It must be payday!"

Sure enough, the reason Rick asked to meet with me, was because the Lord had impressed upon him to give me $1000 in CASH despite the fact that we had agreed that there would be no charge for my help.

He handed me ten crisp, $100 bills and I thanked him and left. He had no idea I was needing that amount. He was just obeying what the Lord had told him. Rick was always like that. So faithful to the Lord and I will always be grateful for his walk with God and kindness to me.

I got in my car and left the subdivision, looking for the first gas station I could find. Within a few miles, I was climbing a gentle hill when the car finally ran out of gas and fumes. I was travelling about 50 miles per hour, and I had enough momentum to crest the hill and begin coasting down the other side.

As it happened, there was a gas station on the right that I was able to glide into and pull up beside the pump. When the attendant came to pump my gas, I handed him a $100 bill and said, "Fill 'er up!"

It was just like God promised. When I literally ran out, He replenished! His faithfulness was becoming a reality to me as I slowly came to terms with the idea that God still loved me and had plans for my life.

The next several months were adventurous to say the least and I ended up in Nashville, TN where I remarried and settled down.

In 2000, I wrote *Selling Among Wolves – Without Joining the Pack!* At the International Christian Bookstore convention in New Orleans, I was invited to be a guest on The 700 Club, but the day of the interview, there was an uprising in Israel, so they ran with that story instead.

I was already there, so they filmed the interview anyway with the intention of airing it the next day. Unfortunately, current events kept knocking me off the schedule until it faded from my mind, and I moved to Florida in 2001.

It had been sixteen years of making a life of trying to fulfill my end of the deal I made with God that cold, rainy day in Canada. I had promised to study His Word and apply it, and if it worked, I would tell everyone about it.

I was disappointed that the vision I had sixteen years earlier of seeing myself on The 700 Club was once again squashed. (They had previously done an interview with me in 1991 for my book, Psalm 91 – The Ultimate Shield, but it never aired due to the sudden end of the Gulf War.)

It was never my goal or dream to be on The 700 Club. I had never asked for that, but I was shown it in the most unusual and unsolicited way, so I always wondered about it. Well, in 2001, I bought what for me at the time, was a dream home by the lake, with a pool and lots of warm sunny weather.

It was the first home I had purchased since selling off my real estate assets to pay bills back in the early '80's. Not only did I feel like I was finally ESTABLISHED again as God promised me, but the day I moved in and began unpacking, the realtor dropped by and said his son called from out of state and said he saw me on television.

"Impossible" I said. "I've been here unpacking all day and haven't done a television interview in months, and the last one I did, didn't even air."

He insisted his son (who I did not know, and I had no idea that he knew I existed) saw me that very morning on television. So that night, the night I was finally being ESTABLISHED again, I plugged in my TV that was sitting on a box and decided to watch the rerun of that day's edition of The 700 Club.

Sure enough, the interview I did with them three months earlier about my new *Selling Among Wolves* book, finally aired and I saw myself being interviewed with my name at the bottom of the screen just like God showed me that lonely, cold, drizzly day sixteen years earlier!

The day in 1985 when I saw myself being interviewed on The 700 Club on someone else's TV when in fact that had never happened, was the same day that He promised me that I would be established again. And the day I was actually reestablished with my own home and took possession of it, was the day, that vision was literally fulfilled. It was a giant exclamation point in my life!

God is so incredibly faithful! And since then, I have been learning more and more of His secrets and enriching the lives of countless thousands with His truths.

I won't live long enough to drain and distill all His secrets, but such as I have and all that I continue to get, I now make available in my mentorship site (ridiculously affordable) and in my LIVE coaching group (ridiculously underpriced). See MichaelPink.com/Secrets for details.

CHAPTER 28

Nice Guys Can (And Should) Finish First

"But I say to you, **love your enemies***, bless those who curse you, do good to those who hate you, and pray for those who spitefully use you and persecute you,"* (Matthew 5:44)

"Behold, I send you out as sheep in the midst of wolves. Therefore be wise as serpents and **harmless as doves***."* (Matthew 10:16)

A Colorado businessman once told me that his business was hurting because he refused to lower his standards and use high pressure, manipulative sales techniques to close business. His competition on the other hand apparently had no scruples and seemed to be prospering despite their use of heavy handed, high pressure "closing" techniques and other questionable selling tactics.

He was beginning to believe the lie that "Nice guys finish last!" He felt he would have to choose between his convictions or profits, as if they were somehow mutually exclusive.

I think nice guys can finish first, but I also think nice guys are people who compete vigorously, though fairly. Being nice does not imply being a doormat. Doormats do finish last! In sales, a nice guy will find ways to "outserve" his competition, not provide mediocre service and complain about the wolves when he loses the sale.

Nice guys excel in providing the best service, the best product, and the most innovative ideas in the most clear, concise and compelling manner. To quote one writer, they don't "flinch in the face of sacrifice, hesitate in the presence of the adversary, negotiate at the table of the enemy, ponder at the pool of popularity, or meander in the maze of mediocrity." Indeed, they function with excellence in the marketplace and are a witness to those around them!

In the case of the Colorado businessman, he needed to learn Biblical principles and strategies adapted to the selling process in a way that he could incorporate into his business. His average sale was just under $1,000, typically a one call close.

Because not every prospect was ready to purchase on the first meeting and because he was a "nice guy", he often walked away empty handed, and his competition would swoop in, not leaving without a signed contract or a police escort!

If I was selling home security systems and my father was a good candidate for one, but wanted some time to think it over, I wouldn't lose the sale to a competitor during the interim no matter how slick, polished or pressuring he was. Why? Because of the rapport (relationship) and the trust I have established with my father.

In fact, even if my product were more expensive than the competition, I would still get the sale. The art of creating trust and developing rapport are an often-overlooked component to making sales and need not be neglected in favor of product knowledge, skill or technique.

To make this point, I need to tell you about a Florida man who once called me stating that he was starting his first job in sales in just a few days. He was scared, unskilled and unprepared to provide for his family on a straight commission job with no guarantees or cash advances.

He was desperate for help and asked me to train him over the phone on how to sell. I explained that the skills he needed would take years to develop and he didn't have that much time. He needed to grasp what I call the four foundational principles of selling and function out of an understanding of those.

His skill would come in time, but it was possible to grasp and begin applying those principles for an immediate impact. He believed me and took copious notes. A week later he called me with the results. He had made eight presentations and secured eight sales for a first week commission check of $3,000!

Needless to say, this man became an ardent believer in my "principle based" approach to sales and continued on in a highly successful career.

Going back to our man in Colorado, he needed to recognize that 90% of the decision to buy is made in the heart and the other 10% is simply the mind needing to justify what the heart wants. In short, he had to learn how to win the battle for the heart.

If he could win that battle, no high-pressure competitor would take that sale away any more than a high-pressure suitor would have convinced my fiancée (now my wife) to marry him instead of me.

So how do we win the battle for the heart? The overriding principle here is to *"serve with all your heart, from the heart, to win the heart".* It's been said that Canaan is a type of the heart or soul, and that Joshua is a type of the born again spirit man.

Joshua went out to subdue and conquer the land of Canaan

under the leadership of the Commander of the host of the Lord, to bring it into subjection to the government of God much like our spirit man in submission to God's Spirit, brings our soul (mind, will and emotions) into subjection to the government (kingdom) of God.

This is a lifelong process that Paul refers to in Romans 12:1 - 2 where he instructs us to *"be not conformed to the world, but be transformed by the renewing of our mind"* and again in Philippians 2:12 - 13 where he instructs us to *"work out your own salvation with fear and trembling.... for God is at work in you"*.

The lessons that can be learned from Joshua's conquest of Canaan can be wonderfully applied to the modern day battles we face in the business arena. We know from Paul's letter to the Corinthians that the things which happened to the children of Israel were an example and shadows of things to come.

Deuteronomy records that there were seven nations that God commanded the Israelites to drive out of Canaan. The etymology of the seven names of those nations corresponds to seven character traits often found in the heart of man that need to be driven out.

For example, the Hittites. Their name means "terror". They occupied the northern fertile crescent of Canaan and had a fearsome reputation for dominating and intimidating their foes. Many people are like that. They're hostile and use intimidation to get what they want.

In sales, they demand price concessions and unreasonable delivery schedules etc. They operate on a win/lose basis. They win. You lose. When you encounter a "Hittite" like person, (one who is openly hostile, intimidating and demanding their own way), you must diffuse their hostility and intimidation before you can develop a fiercely loyal customer.

At the root of their terrorizing antics is their own terror. Their fear of failure. Their fear of rejection. Their fear of being hurt or being taken advantage of.

You may have heard it said that "hurting people, hurt others... healed people, heal others." I would like to submit that terrorized people...terrorize others and confident people...well, they look terror in the face and give them the security they're *really* looking for.

I remember a Canadian businessman I was trying to sell a copier to in 1978. When I walked in the lobby of his office, he walked past and said to the secretary in a rude and gruff voice, "Get rid of him!" I politely declined his offer and walked over to where he was standing in the center of the office.

I believe my boldness surprised him. It did me! When he looked me in the face, I was polite, kind, courteous and confident. He directed me to his controller who later made the purchase from me. My strategy was simple. Minister in the opposite spirit.

He was operating out of fear. I was operating out of boldness that comes from the Lord. He was rude and intimidating. I was polite and engaging. My confidence earned his respect, if not his envy.

My kindness in the face of his rudeness captured a part of his heart and for a moment, he allowed me entrance into his business and life. From there I simply outserved my competitors and easily won the business.

Some say that a nice guy would have left when he told the secretary to get rid of me, but I was too nice to let him purchase what I believed to be an inferior product for a higher price.

I was too nice to let myself become another notch on his belt of salesman he had kicked out of his office and would one day have to answer for. I was too nice to let him get away with being a total jerk that day. Instead, I confronted him with kindness and the love of Christ exhibited with confidence, and it carried the day.

Too often we try to be nicer than Jesus and when we get beaten in the marketplace we blame it on the bad guys, hiding behind our religious platitudes as we make excuses, instead of learning from our mistakes, becoming effective at engaging the culture and leading the market, dare I say dominating the market with a Christian world view that leads through service and knows no surrender but to Christ.

CHAPTER 29

The Mustard Seed Fallacy

"Because of your unbelief (little faith); for assuredly, I say to you, ***if you have faith as a mustard seed****, you will say to this mountain, 'Move from here to there,' and it will move; and nothing will be impossible for you.'"* (Matthew 17:20)

"Make no small plans, for they have no power to stir the soul."

I've heard it a hundred times and so have you… "If you only had the teensiest, itty bitty bit of faith, no bigger than a mustard seed, you could move a mountain into the sea." The obvious point being, that their faith must be microscopic because it can't seem to cure a headache.

But is that the point that Jesus was making? That all it takes is a very small amount of faith to move mountains?

Look at the words of Jesus…
"Why are you fearful, **O you of little faith***?"* (Matthew 8:26) or *"****O you of little faith****, why do you reason among yourselves because you have brought no bread?"* (Matthew 16:8) or *"If then God so clothes the grass, which today is in the field and tomorrow is thrown into the oven, how much more will He clothe you,* **O you of little faith***?"* (Luke 12:28)

Every time Jesus spoke of little faith, it was not a compliment. Does it make sense to you that He would say *"O you of little faith, you too can move mountains."*?

People wrongly believe that Jesus is suggesting that microscopic faith is enough to move mountains. However, smallness of size is not the right characteristic because Jesus never commends small or little faith.

I believe He was He referencing its effect and process, not its size. In some ways, tapping into faith to produce a result is like plugging into the electrical outlet in your home.

Once you've entered the state of electric connection (faith), it will power whatever is attached, be that a toaster, vacuum or television (cure a headache, or meet some other need).

So, perhaps in that sense, once you are "in faith" believing for a particular outcome, it matters not the size of the thing you desire to see moved. Faith will move it.

If not size, what do we compare the mustard seed to?
Jesus said, *"The **kingdom of heaven** is **like** a mustard seed…"*, So we need to think of mustard seed faith to be like the kingdom of Heaven. What is the kingdom of Heaven like?

Jesus went on to explain… *"which indeed is the least of all the seeds;"* (Matthew 13:32) Here Jesus acknowledges (but doesn't commend) its size. When comparing the kingdom of Heaven to a mustard seed, He is saying it starts off small and then grows.

Jesus adds these important words, *"…but when it is grown…"* The nature of faith like a mustard seed, is that it grows and matures. A newborn baby has the same number of muscles as Mr. Universe, but they haven't grown or matured yet, so the baby can't do very much. We need to strengthen our faith by reason of use.

Excellence

Jesus then adds *"...becomes greater than all herbs..."* This is a qualitative statement, more than merely a statement of size. Greatness is not to be shunned. Don't you want your kids to do great?

It was said of Daniel and the three Hebrew children that, *"In all matters of wisdom and understanding about which the king examined them, he found them ten times **better than all who were in his realm.**"* (Daniel 1:20) That description was a positive, not a negative. Aspiring to do well, even ten times better than the world is a good thing.

Then he adds the quantitative phrase... *"shoots out large branches..."* If you're going to be thinking anyway, you might as well think big, whether influence or quality or actual size. If you're going to be believing for something, you may as well believe big. But why?

Jesus finishes His statement with the reason for believing big... *"so that the birds of the air may nest under its shade."* In business terms, this is about providing meaningful value to the market. As James 2:20 says, *"Faith without works is dead."*

Don't look at the physical size of a mustard seed as something to be attained, but rather at what it accomplishes and the process by which it does.

CHAPTER 30

Finding Abundance Right Under Your Nose

*"Break up **your fallow ground**,*
And do not sow among thorns." (Jeremiah 4:3)

*"Break up **your fallow ground**, for it is time to seek the Lord,*
Till He comes and rains righteousness on you." (Hosea 10:12)

Solomon said, *"Much food is in the fallow ground of the poor, and for lack of justice there is waste."* (Proverbs 13:23) When you understand AND act upon the implications of this verse, you will experience life changing increase!

After losing my wife of 24 years and starting over with Judy, I stepped back from active ministry and business. During the next four years our relationship prospered beyond what we imagined, but my business, ministry and website laid pretty much dormant.

Heading into year five, I asked the Lord about why things were so tight. He spoke softly the truth… *"Son, you have let your ground lay fallow."* Instantly, I recalled the Proverb that states, *"There is much food (provision) in the fallow ground of the poor."* Do you hear what that is saying???

Fallow ground by definition, is ground that has been plowed and readied for sowing, but then seed is withheld, and the ground is allowed to lay dormant, and it becomes hard and unproductive. If you're not a farmer, think of fallow ground as anything you have, that was created to yield increase but is not being utilized.

It could be a skill, a gifting, or a talent. It could be a business, a website, an idea you've been sitting on, or something as basic as your sales territory. It could be a specific demographic, a region, or a calling. Anything God has given you that could yield increase if properly and diligently worked!

God says that even the poor have enough "fallow ground" to produce MUCH FOOD. Some translations refer to the potential as "abundance". But the reason the poor or those in a state of lack are often still poor is that they are not working their field. This may not be a work ethic problem. They may not even know they have a field or how to work it.

But because they (we) are not planting, nurturing, watering, or grooming the field God has for us, we are not experiencing harvest. There is usually a little because of the random seeds from prior harvests that have fallen in the ground and grown up, but by and large there is lack.

So, God was gently pointing out to me that the field He has called me to had laid dormant those four years. And if I wanted to see harvests again, I needed to plow that untilled land I had previously worked so hard for so many years. I needed to begin sowing into that field and lending my sweat and labor, my heart and love, to that calling.

So how about you? Are you experiencing lack right now? Are you working your fallow ground? I'm not asking if you're busy. I'm asking if you are working the field, by sowing, watering, laboring, etc. DO NOT confuse activity for productivity. Take a hard look at the metrics that produce a harvest in your line of work. Lay the "story" (excuses) aside and just look at YOUR metrics. Then ask two questions...

1. Are you working in the field He has called you to and prepared you for?

2. Are you performing the metrics at a high enough level to produce a big harvest?

This is just the tip of the iceberg! When you truly grasp the secret of the fallow ground, your life will never be the same again, and lack will not long be your portion!

Some have pointed out that the last half of Proverbs 13:23 *("for lack of justice, there is waste")* reveals that the poor among us are usually exposed to loss and wastage **because of injustice.** While that is certainly true, there is more to that verse than you might think. But first, I want to acknowledge the obvious…

Jesus said that the poor would always be with us. (Mark 14:7) Solomon tells us that he who gives to the poor, lends to the Lord and the Lord will repay. (Proverbs 19:17) Paul and the other apostles were also deliberate and mindful to help the poor. James said that the poor in this world are rich in faith. (James 2:5)

All this to say, that the poor are not to be disregarded or disrespected. They should be helped – even generously. And I would suggest that one of the best ways to help the poor is to lead them out of poverty, not just write them a check. Both are needed, but the first is more needful in the long term.

Having said that, are the poor destined to remain poor, due to injustice? Are they just supposed to accept poverty as their lot in in life because of whatever injustices they may have incurred?

Consider, Booker T. Washington who grew up as a slave in pre-civil war America and only owned one pair of clothes. He gained his freedom and started a school for former slaves. Most students did not even know how to brush their teeth, let alone read or write. His school (Tuskegee Institute) taught Biblical principles and with George Washington Carver's help, Natural Law.

Adding to those foundations, he helped them develop a practical trade, and within 40 years his school produced more self-made millionaires out of former slaves than Harvard, Yale, and Princeton combined, the 3-top schools at the time. So, yes injustice is real, but it doesn't have to define your future.

Here's where it gets interesting… I decided to seek the Lord and study the Hebrew on this verse, particularly about the injustice. Here is what I found…

The word often translated as injustice or lack of justice in this verse is the Hebrew word "mishpat" which is derived from "shawfat" (Strong's 8199) which means to judge, but in its broader meaning, it means to govern. A more literal interpretation of this verse would read… *"Abundance of food is in the tillage of the poor, but it is swept away and consumed by lack of judgment or governance."*

Think about that… the loss of resources or lack of success can often be attributed to our own lack of judgment or lack of personal governance. We are talking about personal responsibility here!

The preceding verse, *"A good man leaves an inheritance to his children's children, but the wealth of the sinner is stored up for the righteous."* (Proverbs 13:22) bears this out by contrasting those with good judgment and governance with the sinner who has none. It points out that a good man leaves an inheritance to his children's children, but the wealth of the sinner is laid up for the just. Verse 23 is simply a continuation of the same idea.

This is not to say there's no injustice in the world because that abounds, but when properly understood, this verse urges personal responsibility for a way out of our condition. We are not responsible for what circumstance we arrived at in this world, but we are responsible for how we respond to those circumstances.

We suffer loss, not because of injustice many times, but rather because of our own poor judgment or refusal to govern ourselves and our spending, etc. We suffer loss sometimes simply because we refuse to throw off the yoke of injustice and prefer to remain a victim.

Others just accept their condition as their lot in life, but it need not be. Still others desperately want out, but don't know the path to success. That is what www.MichaelPink.com/Secrets is all about… Leading the way out.

Here's the deal… If you want to get great increase from your fallow ground (and we all have plenty of that), you must FIRST take personal responsibility for how you have responded to whatever circumstance you are in.

Where or when did you suffer loss due to lack of knowledge? (Hosea 4:6) Where have you lacked good judgment? Where did you proceed without even asking God to give you His judgment, His perspective, His great wisdom on the matter?

What was informing your judgment? Was it a hot tip from the cab driver? What is greed or covetousness? Perhaps obtaining wealth without contributing real value? Prayerfully review your prior lack of judgment to its root and expose it to the light of God's Truth. Repent. Turn away from that way of thinking in the future.

Where were you guided by poor personal governance, which is another way of saying lack of personal discipline or self-control? Do you even attempt to live a disciplined life as a disciple of Jesus Christ?

Look at your consumption, your waste of time or goods, or anything that demonstrates a lack of restraint. A little honey is good, but too much will make you vomit (Proverbs 25:16).

The first step to success is the rejection of evil. Romans 12:9 tells us to *"abhor evil and cling to good."* Romans 12:2 tells us to *"be transformed by the renewing of our mind"*, but renewing anything such as a house for example, requires tearing out the bad and then replacing it with good. Deal with the bad first. Then go to work on rebuilding your future! Otherwise, you're just painting over rotten wood.

Maybe it's time to look at what caused a lot of loss in your life and don't blame it on the wicked, even if they did cheat you. Where were the checks and balances (governance)? Where was the judgment? I am not saying that bad outcomes are always our fault, but I am saying they are not always someone else's fault.

Regardless of who is to blame, in the end, we need to acknowledge where we are at, reject the notion of staying down, repair the breach and get back in the race!

CHAPTER 31

The Rule of Three for More Effective Communication

*"Have I not written to you excellent **(threefold)** things of counsels and knowledge, that I may make you know the certainty of the words of truth, that you may answer words of truth to those who send to you?"* (Proverbs 22:20-21)

*"And now **these three remain**: faith, hope and love. But the greatest of these is love."* (1 Corinthians 13:13)

*"And there are **three that bear witness** on earth: the Spirit, the water, and the blood; and these **three agree as one**."* (1 John 5:8)

When Solomon wrote in Proverbs 22:20, *"Have not I written to you excellent things of counsels and knowledge"* the word translated as "excellent" means "threefold" or "triad". At its root, a triad is a "group or set of three connected people or things".

He went on to explain that the reason he spoke in threes or threefold things (which are indeed excellent), was so that we could know the certainty of the truths he spoke and so we could provide truth to those who ask us questions.

It has long been known, but seldom understood that there is something highly efficacious, totally satisfying and utterly desirable about the number three as it relates to communication, structure, and visual imagery.

The rule of three is an effective communication device that suggests that a trio of features or benefits, events or characters, ideas or thoughts is somehow more humorous, satisfying, or memorable than other numbers.

The number three combines the need for brevity and the pleasure of rhythm with the least amount of information needed to create a recognizable pattern.

Also, research shows that we can recall just three to four items from our short-term memory with ease. That's why phone numbers are broken into a 3-digit area code, followed by a 3-digit prefix, followed by the last 4 numbers. Much easier to remember.

The Scripture is replete with groupings of three. Father, Son and Holy Spirit come to mind. The number three communicates completeness in an irreducible way. Before the flood, there were three righteous patriarchs, (Abel, Enoch and Noah). After the flood, we hear often about the God of Abraham, Isaac and Jacob.

We know that Jesus prayed three times in the Garden of Gethsemane, was placed on the cross on the 3rd hour of the day (9 AM) and died at the 9th hour (3 PM) followed by 3 hours of darkness, and three full days and three full nights in the grave.

For reasons that may not be clear, we feel a sense of completeness when information is presented in threes. A three-point sermon for example. We learn our A, B, C's not our A, B, C, and D's or our A, B's. We'll say, one, two, three – GO! Or… On your mark… Get set… GO!

In literature we read about the Three Blind Mice, Three Musketeers, Three Little Pigs, etc. How many times have you heard, "Hear No Evil, See No Evil, Do No Evil" from the Three Wise Monkeys?

The US Declaration of Independence famously proclaims: Life, Liberty, and the Pursuit of Happiness. Abraham Lincoln in his Gettysburg Address said, "We cannot dedicate, we cannot consecrate, we cannot hallow this ground… government of the people, by the people, for the people."

Martin Luther King closed his famous "I Have a Dream" speech with "Free at last. Free at last. Thank God almighty, we are free at last." Julius Caesar gave a speech no one remembers except this one sentence… "Veni, Vidi, Vici" (I came, I saw, I conquered.)

The number three is used some 467 times in the Bible, but my friend, Pastor Tim Nicholson in Wichita, KS, a devout student of Scripture and a fierce warrior for the cause and love of Christ has catalogued over 1,500 threefold groupings or expressions in the Bible.

When I began studying the Tabernacle of Moses, I noticed there were 3 colors of thread, 3 types of metal, 3 sections in the tabernacle itself and more I could mention. Here are just a very few examples of threes in the Bible…

Outer Court	**Inner Court**	**Holy of Holies**
Natural light	Candlelight	Supernatural light
Holy Spirit	Son	Father
Body	Soul	Spirit
Prophet	Priest	King
Way	Truth	Life
Milk of the Word	Bread of the Word	Meat of the Word
30-fold increase	60-fold increase	100-fold increase
Faith	Hope	Love
Knowledge	Wisdom	Understanding

In business, especially when communicating, group your main ideas and your most salient points in groupings of three if you want them to be remembered. Back in the mid-nineties, I heard an interview with Jay Abraham, one of the leading marketing experts in America. I found his talk absolutely riveting. Not just because what he said made sense, but he delivered his message in bursts of three.

Every concept, every strategy, and every tactic he described seemed to have a three-dimensional aspect to it, that when heard and understood, created a fourth, unseen dimension that riveted his concepts to my consciousness as quickly and securely as a mechanic changing tires on a race car at the Indy 500!

Naturally, the content needs to be useful, relevant, and valuable if the listener is going to be subconsciously motivated to take hold of your threefold grouping mentally and emotionally, but if it is, then your message will be remembered.

Often in sales, the person you're speaking with will either need or want the approval of someone else, be that their spouse, their business partner, or their boss. If your value proposition can be summed up in their mind with something like, "His new ABC process is faster, better and cheaper" and understands why that is so, they are much more likely to gain the approval they seek.

I don't know why God made it that way, but He did, and you will find that your communications will have more impact, more heat, and more sizzle when you tap into the mystery, power, and completeness of three.

Last Word

Your journey is just beginning.

There is a vast difference between being informed and truly being transformed. Hopefully with this book, you've been informed in such a way as to awaken the desire to be transformed. (Romans 12:2)

The latter is a process and requires walking away from the subconsciously engrained habits that call to us like an echo resounding with a comfortable familiarity to "go with what we know", to stay within the bounds of the accepted norms of the world we grew up in and even loved.

Staying within the bounds of the world, enforced by the tyranny of the status quo, carries with it a promise of acceptance. And we all want acceptance. But friendship with the world is enmity with God. (James 4:4) Many choose the path of the world, the status quo, because they crave and prefer the praise of men more than the praise of God. (John 12:43). Others just find it to be an easier path.

But the ways of the world and all it has to offer are temporary in nature (2 Corinthians 4:18). It's so easy to just go with the flow downstream towards the same destination as the masses, but the reward is upstream at the source of the river.

It's that crystal clear mountain lake, that reservoir of pure Word (Jesus) where new life is birthed and released to interact with the world and change it. To be the salt of the earth and the light of the world. That's our destiny. Our privilege, even our calling.

Yes, it is a challenge to swim upstream against the prevailing currents. You may be mocked and ridiculed and falsely accused, but as Jesus said in Matthew 5:12, *"Rejoice and be exceedingly glad, for great is your reward in heaven..."*

When I first became a Christian, my coworkers would taunt and mock and laugh at me. I was sport to them. I wasn't obnoxious. I didn't preach to them. I just didn't cave to their ways. I stood out.

A few years later as a young copier salesman, I was sent away for a week of sales training with six or eight other sales reps from other offices around British Columbia. Sitting at dinner one night in the hotel restaurant, one of the "cool" sales reps asked everyone to reveal what horoscope sign they went by.

One by one, the various reps stated their sign (Taurus, Libra, Virgo, etc.) When it came to me, and not wanting to even appear to go along with this practice of astrology, I stated that I went by the sign of the cross.

You could have cut the air with a knife.

They were thinking... WHAT did he just say?!?!?!?

They insisted I tell them what my astrological sign was, but I played ignorant (even though I knew).

It was a very uncomfortable moment for me. I wanted to be liked and accepted just like you, but I was not willing to conform to the ways of the world to gain that acceptance.

Later that night, one of the salesmen approached me privately. As it turned out, he admired my bold stand for Jesus. It convicted him, and he wanted what I had. He gave his life to Jesus that night. And shortly after that, he introduced me to his brother who was also a salesman there and he too, gave his life to Christ.

By simply choosing to not conform to the ways of the world, two men were inspired to make a decision that would change their life forever and perhaps the lives of countless others who they would later influence in the years to come.

One of the things that gave me courage to be bold, was the support I had at the branch office where I worked. The branch manager and a couple other employees were Christians and we had weekly Bible study and prayer.

The opportunity to interact with other believers who wanted to grow in their walk with Jesus and learn His ways made an incredible difference for all of us. Not only did we win dozens to Christ, but we also excelled with the best performance of any branch in the company.

One Year Online Course & Membership Group
Because I know so few have that kind of Biblical support, we've created an online community where you can grow in your faith and acquire Biblical skills for excelling in the marketplace. It's where you go from merely being informed to being transformed with other like-minded believers.

It's where the things you've read in this book (and much more) **are taught with the other three books in this series, in a ONE-YEAR ONLINE COURSE, with LIVE discussion and group interaction so the wisdom you discover can ultimately be etched into the way you operate in this world.**

It's your new operating system enabling you to provide well for your family, advance God's kingdom, and be a witness to the nations!

It's a modest monthly membership (with no contract) where the truths you read about in God's Best Kept Secrets are expanded into a weekly curriculum format with audio teaching and LIVE monthly meetups and other surprises to discuss your progress, answer your questions and get you living the life you've always wanted to live!

There are also several other courses on specific topics like sales and business development that have been sold for thousands of dollars but are FREE as part of your monthly membership.

I'd love to have you in the group, and together we can make an impact in this world that desperately needs the hope that lays within you! Go to MichaelPink.com/Secrets where you can **GET YOUR FIRST MONTH FOR JUST $1**.